Strength of the Spirit

**One Woman's Journey Toward Health and Enlightenment
Through Her Ten-year Battle with Cancer**

Beth Carpenter, N. D.

Strength of the Spirit

Published by: Violet Crown Publishing
                  P. O. Box 3107
                  Austin, Texas 78764

First Printing 1999

ISBN 0-9670836-0-5
Cover illustration by Bart Sharp (512) 458-1352
                  1800 Romford
                  Austin, Tx 78704

Disclaimer: The author of this book wishes to make it clear that she does not dispense medical advice or prescribe the use of any technique as a form of treatment for medical problems without the advice of a physician, either directly or indirectly. The author is not a physician or a psychologist and is not trying to portray herself as one in any way. The author is a Life Science Educator and a Consultant of Natural Health. Nothing in this book is for the purpose of diagnosing, treating, alleviating, mitigating, curing, preventing, or caring for "disease" in any way or manner whatsoever. All teachings and methods in this book are for the sole purpose of assisting people to learn how to build their own health. In the event you use any of the information in this book for yourself, you are prescribing for yourself, which is your constitutional right, but the author and publisher assume no responsibility for your actions.

Printed in the United States of America

ACKNOWLEDGMENTS

Through the constant loving support of my family and friends I was able to complete this book. Not only did they encourage me in writing this book, but they also offered a helping hand while I was sick. I especially wish to acknowledge the following people: my mother Carolyn Trower; my stepfather Bob Trower; my grandparents Ralph and Betty Shannon; my siblings, Deborah Voorhees, Glen Voorhees, Becky and Billy Coury, and Robyn Porter; my father and stepmother Glen and Mikey Voorhees, my nana Helen Voorhees; Laurice Crumley; Jerry Carpenter; Jack Carpenter; the graveyard shift at Eldorado Hotel & Casino; Reva Dark; Cathy Wagner; James Furrh; Tanya Chuoke; Mr. and Mrs. Fry; DeeDee Garrison; Sherri Rice; Chuck Holt; Judge C. L. Ray; Scott Weiss, D.C.; Connie Arismende; Tanzy Maxfield; the Child Assault Prevention Program (CAPP); Robin Heart Shepperd, D.C.; and my partner, Tim Cross.

I want to extend a very special acknowledgment to my doctor, Dr. James Forsythe, and his entire staff especially Valerie and Beverly. I would like to acknowledge Dr. Daniel Flynn, Stanford University Hospital, and the Bone Marrow Transplant team members for their dedication and love of their work, and especially Dr. Blume and Dr. Long.

Thanks to my office assistant, Barbara Newitt; my editors, Raymond Borrego, Melanie Middleton and Kam Magor, and Bart Sharp for the design, the dedication, and the cover artwork, and Carrie Cox for typesetting the book.

TABLE OF CONTENTS

Foreword

by James Forsythe, M.D., H.M.D.

This story exemplifies the sheer power and self-determination of one individual fighting for her life against a killer which has taken the life of such famous people as Jackie Kennedy and recently King Hussein. These individuals with all of their wealth and resources, using only conventional medicine, lost the battle for life, whereas Beth with her desperate search for answers, using a combination of alternative and integrative therapies along with carefully administered chemotherapy and ultimately a successful bone-marrow transplant, was able to survive her illness and be alive almost ten years without relapse.

The pivotal factor in this story is the fact that Beth never gave up despite many setbacks both in her personal and financial life, but also in the relapsing course of her illness. She doggedly searched for ways to build her immune system with antioxidants, herbs, vitamins, minerals as well as detoxification of her colon and liver and improved nutrition, and the natural use of vital chemicals.

These vital chemicals are present in fresh or lightly steamed vegetables such as cabbage, carrots, cauliflower, beans, broccoli, and brussels sprouts, as well as in fresh juicing. Juicing is an important aspect of immune fortification and should not be overlooked. Additionally, Beth incorporated daily exercise and positive thinking. She excluded from consciousness negative feelings and used humor to heal. The personal support of her mother earlier in her disease, and later her husband, was another important and not to be overlooked aspect in her winning equation.

In retrospect, I learned much from Beth as I do and should all doctors from their special patients. I saw in Beth a unique courage and fierce determination, and yes there were tears at times, but she had the fortitude to eventually be victorious over her cancer.

In my own background, I was trained in a strictly conventional manner and then in the subspecialty of Medical Oncology at the University of California, San

Francisco in the early 1970's. I also had a strong background in pathology and internal medicine as well as serving in Vietnam as Chief of Tropical Diseases and Blood Banking in 1969. I reflected back on medical school, and after four years of classes, less than four hours were devoted to nutrition. diet, vitamins, herbs, and minerals. The term homeopathy or naturopathy was never once mentioned in the four-year curriculum. Thanks to the successes of alternative medicine, alternative medicine electives are now offered in over fifty percent of all medical school curricula.

To my knowledge, there are only two homeopathic oncologists in the United States today, and I am one of them. I decided fifteen years ago to keep an open mind and understand the natural healing arts. Thanks to my persistence in this area, and despite some questioning comments from peers and colleagues, I have been able to establish a thriving practice in this area and have been able to do so without impedance from the Nevada Medical Board.

Afterall, medicine is both science and art, and if the art of medicine is lost, the kind of success story which happened with Beth would rarely occur, and certainly never come to us in such a heartfelt biography.

"There is no chance, no destiny, no fate,
Can circumvent, or hinder, or control
The firm resolve of a determined soul.
Gifts count for nothing; WILL alone is great;
All things give way before it, soon or late,
What obstacle can stay the mighty force
of the sea-seeking river in its course,
Or cause the ascending orb of day to wait?

Each well-born soul must win what it deserves.
Let the fool prate of luck. The fortunate
Is he whose earnest purpose never swerves,
Whose slightest action or inaction serves
The one great aim.
Why, even Death stands still,
And waits an hour sometimes for such a WILL."

–Ella Wheeler Wilcox

Introduction

Close your eyes, place your hand over your heart and see the flame that burns within your very soul. Know that you can have anything you desire.

• • • • •

During the years I was battling cancer many people encouraged me to write and tell my story, but I thought I had nothing to offer in helping people with their struggles. However, after succeeding in my ten year challenge with cancer, I finally came to the conclusion that I had something to share. I'm going to tell you everything that I did in my healing process, and I hope that in reading my story, you, too, can find courage and healing along your life's path. Through my ten year journey toward regaining my health, I explored and experimented with both alternative and traditional approaches in hopes of becoming whole and well.

My cancer experience allowed me to open to a wealth of knowledge and freedom that I would not have otherwise experienced. I combined many methods like ingredients in a recipe to create the perfect solution for me, and that is what each of you will need to do to take control in your own lives. When we do not allow ourselves to see that we have choices, a sense of helplessness takes over, leaving us feeling as if we have no course of action. There's a song by the Eagles, *I'm Already Gone*, which says, "We live our lives in chains never even knowing we hold the key." This is really true! We do hold the key to all of our answers, but we have to open our eyes, ears, and senses so that we can be receptive to the answers that are always waiting to be discovered.

Through my experimentation, I found some methods to

be more successful than others, but everything I did was right for me. Everything you do will be right for you, too. There's a saying that states, "If you knew better, you'd do better," and through knowing more, you will continue to change, grow and perfect your journey in life. It's along this path that you tap into a never-ending well of information and knowledge, which, when available, can open up more opportunities. This knowledge comes not only from outside of us, but also from inside each one of us. Remember in creating your perfect life recipe that it's good to continue to add new ingredients so that life doesn't become stale.

I do hope in living your life that you shed a few tears and laugh a few laughs. My life seems to be filled with tears and laughter, and I wish the same for yours. Find humor in every turn and know you will be all right, and when you feel pain, let the tears flow as you cry and scream. Don't hold it in; release the pain. Life is about the journey, not about the destination; so if you're waiting to be happy only after you've reached your goal, please stop and take a deep breath, and then start living now.

I now know that everything I experienced was meant to give me the necessary knowledge to bring hope and a sense of control into both my life and into others' lives. No matter how chaotic it can sometimes seem, never lose your control. Remember, you're the captain of your ship. By this I mean that you have choices within every situation even when you think that you don't. These choices are within your control.

For example, it's okay to change doctors if you don't like your current doctor. That doctor or health care professional is working for you and should treat your decisions with respect. Find the perfect health care professional for you and then combine this with as many other techniques as you need to create the perfect path of healing for yourself.

To be well you must heal the body, mind, and spirit, and

this means facing fears. By facing your fears you reclaim yourself and disempower the fear. HEALTH, HAPPINESS, and an endless supply of LOVE are our birthright, so I hope that you will claim yours. I have! By bringing into your life this health, happiness and love, you will find success. God bless every one of you.

Chapter 1

Shamrock Stables

Millions of spiritual creatures walk the earth unseen,
both when we wake and when we sleep.
—John Milton, Paradise Lost, IV

Although divine or angelic powers had saved my tail many times, this time they demanded my attention.

Shamrock Stables was always filled during the racing season. The stables, located right outside Hot Springs, Arkansas, board and exercise some of the finest thoroughbreds in the country during the annual spring races. In 1979, my friend Silver and I kept the stables clean, fed the horses, and did whatever else needed to be done. One day I had just finished working a twelve-hour shift and, as always at the end of a shift, was exhausted. However, this day I had decided I was through shoveling manure and was going back to Dallas. I asked for a $50 advance on my paycheck and loaded up my red Ranchero to head home.

It was springtime, and the air was crisp. Even though the days were getting longer, the sun still set early. I picked up Highway 270, a two-lane blacktop, in Hot Springs and headed home for Dallas. Somewhere along Highway 270, between Hot Springs and Catherine, Arkansas, I fell asleep at the wheel. I don't know how long I was asleep, but I do remember waking up. The front end of my Ranchero was under an eighteen-wheeler. When I looked up out of my passenger window I could see that the front half of my

Ranchero was in the left lane under the middle section of the eighteen-wheeler headed back towards Hot Springs. Its rear wheels were within inches of crushing me. I was in a daze.

What happened next I'm not really sure, but, Poof!, the next thing I knew I was driving on the highway still headed for the Texas border, and I could see the semi in my rear-view mirror going the opposite direction.

Why was I saved? Was this Divine Intervention? And, if so, why did I receive the help? What did the universe have in store for me? I found myself frightened and numbed, knowing that I couldn't ignore this event, but I wasn't willing to tell anyone for fear of their disbelief. Confused, I wouldn't talk about this to anyone until thirteen years later, but I would think and wonder about it often.

Chapter 2

On the Edge

All I have to offer anyone is my own experience of the truth.
—Anonymous, *Courage to Change*

Let us first understand the facts, and then we may seek the cause.
—Aristotle

Many people seem to live more than one lifetime within this life, and that is what has happened in my life. The experience with the semi definitely shaped and molded me and helped prepare me for what was to follow.

A few years later, after that angelic intervention, I was running wild and free in Dallas. It was December of 1982, and I was 23 years old. I was living life in the fast lane of drugs, sex, and rock-n-roll. If I was up before the sun went down, it was because I had not gone to sleep. Sometimes I didn't sleep for many days. The majority of my friends were rebels or outlaws. I had to stay on the edge; otherwise, life was boring. However, I was consistent with getting my annual pap smear and vaginal exam so I could get refills on my birth control pills. This year was no exception. I had chosen a new doctor, who required more extensive testing. Other doctors I had in the past would just do the exam and give me my prescription. This one ordered a blood test.

The blood test results showed some abnormalities. The doctor wanted me to come in for further testing, but I didn't have the money. Besides, it was the holiday season, and I was young and immortal. I believed that bad things happened only to other people.

Right after New Year's I began thinking about going in for further testing. After having spent an afternoon with me, a girlfriend, Becky, noticed that the left side of my neck was swollen. I looked in the mirror and, yep, there was a huge swelling under my chin on the left side. I watched it for a few days to see if the swelling would go down, but it didn't. I decided to lay off the drugs. Something was crying for my attention here, but I was trying to stay cool about the whole thing.

Over the next few weeks I felt myself moving in a whirlwind; life became fuzzy. Through my daze I obtained a clinic card as a charity patient at Parkland Hospital, a county hospital and trauma center in Dallas.

Dealing with Parkland was a trauma in itself. People entered in in a steady stream with anything you could imagine – gunshot wounds, stabbings, beatings, car wrecks and, of course, the unknowns. The staff was often buried in blood, guts, and paperwork. It would take the best of people on the best of days to stay cheerful through this; mostly their staff was tired and cranky. I'm not even sure how I kept going; it was as if someone else was in control, and I was just putting one foot in front of the other. It was becoming apparent something was terribly wrong.

My boyfriend, James, and I would meet my mother at the hospital where we would wait amidst the stench and decay. We would wait for hours just to see a doctor, and then, when we did see one, he would begin running tests. The testing seemed endless. There never seemed to be an answer or solution to the swelling in my throat. I was even tested for Cat Scratch Fever. I didn't even know this was a disease; I thought it was only words to a song. I began to lose track of how many tests were run on me. I just wanted it to end soon. I was getting a little cranky, so I began walking into the doctors' private offices and lounges and telling them I was tired of waiting. This actually seemed to help some; the doctors became more attentive and would get to me quicker.

The doctors often stopped and gathered in their huddles to discuss "my situation." Their huddling would begin another round of testing. This went on from January to April '83. My case became the talk of the board meetings. It was finally decided that I should go in for a biopsy, since none of the tests so far had given them a diagnosis. The exploratory surgery was scheduled for April 13, 1983. This test would determine whether the swollen area was a tumor and, if so, whether it was malignant or benign.

Chapter 3

Exploratory Surgery

In my end is my beginning.
—Motto of Mary Queen of Scots

The day of the surgery came quickly enough. I was there early. I had followed my doctor's instructions of no food or water after midnight the night before. My grandparents, my mother, and James were rallying at my side.

There seemed to be some more papers that needed to be signed prior to surgery. The papers said, in a nutshell, that the doctors could do what ever they wanted once they got inside my body. I argued with the staff, telling them that the doctors had my permission to remove only the tumor and nothing else. After much debate and their agreement to comply, I signed my name.

My mother stayed with me until I was wheeled into surgery. I was terrified. The nurse had come in with a pre-op shot, which took effect quickly. I remember being conscious but unable to speak or move. Next thing I knew, the orderly came to take me to my destination. He must have been a kamikaze pilot because he was speeding down the corridors, bumping into other patients on gurneys and taking corners like he was on skates. I thought surely I was going to throw up. I finally landed in the operating room. I thought, "Thank God," but then a nurse came up to me and grabbed my hand. She said to the orderly, "This patient doesn't have a broken hand, and she's not a black male. She's not scheduled for this OR." I was trying not to lose consciousness – I had to communicate with these people and get out of the hands of this idiot! He returned me to where I had begun, and the orderly who was to pick me up was standing there wondering where I had gone. I must have relaxed because the last thing I remember after that was fighting with the oxygen mask that was placed over my face and hearing the nurse say that I had to keep it on. This was also the first thing I remembered coming out from under anesthesia. I was pulling at the mask, feeling that I was suffocating, and the nurse was telling me to keep it on. I don't even remember how long I was in the hospital, but I do remember trying to get that mask off.

When I first woke up, I learned that the surgery had taken five hours, a lot longer than the hour and a half that my family and I had been told. When I was wheeled to my room, my mother and boyfriend were the only ones remaining. My grandparents had to leave because my grandmother had become so nervous she developed diarrhea. The story of how my grandmother washed her panties out and hung them out to dry from one of the hospital windows served as a much needed dose of humor. My grandparents decided that it was best to return home and wait for my mother's phone call.

For the first few days after surgery I couldn't talk, and when my voice did begin to come back, it was hoarse and raspy. As much as I disliked the hospital and some of the doctors, I am very grateful to the surgeon. He told me that he worked extremely hard to save my vocal chords, but he was not sure if my voice would return to normal. I believed that my voice would come back, but sometimes I wasn't sure since a couple of weeks went by before it began showing any real improvement. Thank heaven my voice did return to normal.

The surgeon explained that he would not give me a

diagnosis until the cross-section freeze returned from the lab in a week. That was probably the longest week of my life. I wanted to remain positive, but the fact that the surgery had taken so long was making me anxious about the test results. The diagnosis was given to me on April 21, 1983: poorly differentiated small-cell lymphoma, fourth stage. What did this mean? What was the next step?

The doctors explained that the next step was to see if the disease had spread to my bone marrow through a test known as bone-marrow aspiration. I did not have a clue as to what this meant, and I now know this is one of the most barbaric tests on the face of this planet. Please ask for drugs if you ever have to undergo a bone-marrow aspiration. The doctors and nurses told me it would hurt, but only for a moment, and that it would be over in a flash. It is amazing how much time exists in a "flash." The doctor gave me three shots of Novocaine. One deadened the skin, another deadened the muscle, and the third deadened the outside of the bone. All of these shots hurt, and there is nothing to numb the pain inside the bone while the marrow is being aspirated. After the three shots had numbed their specific areas, the doctor began to insert a long needle-like screw into my hip. My marrow was then aspirated (drawn or sucked out) into the needle, while additional marrow clung to the outside of the needle. The pain was excruciating. My mother was holding my head and saying that it would be over soon and that she loved me. In addition, there seemed to be three or more staff members holding me down while I was crying and screaming. The doctor said that he couldn't get the amount that he needed in one try and asked to go back in a second time. "Hurry!" I yelled. My screams became louder and sounded more animal than human. My leg was paralyzed; I couldn't move my right side. The doctor said they still did not have enough marrow and asked to go in a third time. I told them that they had enough marrow and that they better be extremely careful carrying it to the lab, because they wouldn't be getting any more.

My next visit was to get the results of the bone marrow aspiration. The doctors told me that the disease was in the marrow and that I should follow the set protocol for this incurable disease. The outlined protocol was to begin chemotherapy, progress to radiation, and conclude with a bone-marrow transplant. My mind was reeling; everything was moving too quickly. *What do I do?* I believed they would kill me if I followed this protocol. I said to them, "No, I absolutely will not make a decision or even think about complying at this time, but I would like a prescription of tranquilizers so I can think things through." The doctors were furious, but they gave me the requested prescription.

We left the hospital, and I asked my mom to stop at the nearest pharmacy to have my prescription filled; I wanted a tranquilizer now. My mother stopped at the nearest pharmacy, in a gay neighborhood, and my boyfriend went inside to get the prescription while my mother tried to comfort me in the car. I was crying, wailing, and moaning. My mother was kissing me and holding my face, telling me everything would be all right, when a women walked by and saw us. She just knew we were lesbians and stopped to give us the most indignant look. Her thoughts and expressions were so clear to us that we burst out laughing. To this day, this woman probably has no idea how much tension was released in the belly laugh that she helped us experience.

I was tired of doctors and hospitals, but mostly I was just sick and tired of being sick and tired. It seemed that every time I arrived at the hospital I'd get sick to my stomach and throw up. I didn't know what I wanted to do, but I knew I wasn't going to follow the outlined protocol. I remained firm in my commitment to avoid the transplant and my wishes prevailed. Later my mother and grandparents told me that I was denied the transplant because as the doctors put it, I was "too far gone." This suited me just fine because I was absolutely not going to undergo chemotherapy, radiation, and a bone-marrow transplant. I felt that the doctors just wanted to make a guinea pig out of me. I was angry, numb, and scared.

Chapter 4

Wake-up Call

To remove a mountain, one must
begin with one rock at a time.
−Chinese Proverb

First cleanse the inside of the cup and
then the whole cup will be clean.
−Matthew 23:26

James took me into our neighborhood health food store, described my condition to the clerk and asked if there was anything that would help me. The clerk told us about the therapeutic properties of vitamin C, and how, according to Linus Pauley, a Noble Peace Prize winner, no one would die of a disease if they were taking 10 grams of vitamin C a day. James purchased a large bottle of powdered vitamin C, and I took it mixed in fruit juice four to five times a day until I reached bowel tolerance, about 10,000 mg. Just this one simple change was definitely improving my energy, but I knew there was much more to do.

I felt as if an angel had placed its hand upon my shoulder, reassuring me that I was not alone. This angelic protection gave me a sense of security and hope.

I began seeing a therapist, a friend of my mother's, to try to work some things out in my mind. James had even seen her, upon my request, to help him deal with the crisis. Yes, he went, but the only thing James would say was that he should have the disease instead of me because he was old and worthless. (He was seventeen years my senior.) A whole course of events had been set into motion with the onset of my disease, and James was much too traumatized to stay in relationship and help. We parted ways with no harsh feelings, and over the next few years we would speak from time to time. We both knew that because I had made the decision to heal, that this was where our paths separated.

My mother's support for my cause was building; she was like a mother bear protecting her young. She told me that I had to take a stand or die, and she begged me to consider a nutritional program as alternative treatment. She went into high gear as she began investigating various programs. Almost daily my mother would call or come by with a barrage of new information. If I didn't like the programs, I would say no. Momma would go back out and continue looking. With her third such attempt, I agreed to try one of the programs. Upon my agreement, Momma made me promise to commit to the program for thirty days – one whole month. If I did not feel better at that time, I could choose to do as I wished.

I remember quite vividly the day we went for the initial consultation. Momma picked me up at my apartment as we headed off to Plano, Texas, just north of Dallas, where Mr. & Mrs. Fry lived and ran what was known as the Reams program (I called it the "Doc Reams Program"), which had been developed by a Dr. Reams in Arizona. The Frys tested my urine and saliva to set up the perfect vitamin program for me. I would also follow a strict dietary program. Some of the nutritional aspects were not completely foreign because my mother and her husband had tried to introduce me to a healthier lifestyle when I was in high school. Obviously I hadn't been following any part of it.

With plan in hand, we left the Frys. I was hungry, so we

stopped at Furr's Cafeteria to eat. My mother felt the cafeteria would be a good immediate solution to getting vegetables in me, but I had already made my mind up that this was my last "real" supper. She never said a word as I piled my tray with chicken-fried steak, mashed potatoes and gravy, creamed corn, coleslaw, macaroni and cheese, and German chocolate cake. My mother recalls that there were also three more desserts and numerous other food items. My mother honored my need as I ate to my heart's content. After that meal I faltered only one other day, but otherwise I stayed on the Reams program for three years.

The program began. It called for no meat, no nuts, no berries, no white processed grains (white flour or white rice, aka white by-products) and no other processed foods. For eight months I ate only foods that were easily digested so that my body's energy could be used for healing. I wasn't allowed berries because the little seeds were not easily digested and would get stuck in the crevices of the intestinal wall. I could have four ounces of cheese a week, but nothing processed like American or Velveeta. I could have cheddar, Monterey jack, Colby, provolone, etc. I drank from eight to sixteen ounces of fresh juice a day, fresh meaning it had to be consumed within fifteen minutes of being juiced so that the highest amount of beneficial nutrients would still be there. The juices were always a combination of carrot and celery with occasional beet and or parsley. I ate fruit salads, vegetable salads, steamed vegetables, various types of brown and wild rice, grains such as millet and various types of beans, especially lentils. My mother fixed a lentil loaf probably once a week for quite a while. My family members were extremely supportive. I was eating most of my meals at their house. To make everything easier on me, my mother would not permit my siblings or stepfather to eat anything different, and if they wanted to eat "normal" or "junk" food, they had to eat it elsewhere. My diet consisted of about eighty percent raw food and twenty percent cooked foods.

My routine also included parasite cleanses twice a year to rid my body of any other life forms eating the nutrition meant for me. After the first parasite cleanse, which was about a month into the program, I began my first three-day fast. The fasting was nothing but water, and I did about three of these water fasts, but they were quite difficult for me, so I soon switched to juice fasts, using watermelon juice or carrot juice. Even though with juice fasting you can go much longer than three days, I chose to keep it at three days because I didn't want to release too many toxins at one time. My body responded much better with the juice fasts. I discovered fasting to be one of the best ways to quickly eliminate toxins from my body, as shown in the tarry consistency and frequency of my bowel movements.

When I was fasting the first few days were the most difficult because I was always hungry. I didn't want to move around a lot – I was not only hungry but also dizzy. I would spend the first couple of days on the couch watching rented movies or cable television because watching commercial television when fasting was too hard. Most of the commercials are of food, the most delicious food you think you've ever seen. My mother again rallied support by not allowing anyone to cook anything in the house when I was fasting.

One time I had just started a fast and it was late afternoon or early evening; I thought I was the only one in the house until I smelled popcorn. My mother's husband had come home and had made himself some popcorn. I was upstairs and this aroma filled the whole house, and I began salivating. I was unable to control myself and ran downstairs and began putting anything and everything that was healthy food in my mouth from popcorn to natural candy. I could not get enough food fast enough. Luckily this was the only time I went into an out-of-control feeding frenzy.

If you would like to try fasting, educate yourself about the many types of fasts, and use the one that is best for you and your body. During the summer my personal favorite is the watermelon fast, and during other times of the year I prefer vegetable juice fasts. The watermelon is easy to prepare, but it's very time consuming, so it is helpful to have a second person assisting you. Just cut up the watermelon and throw it in the blender with a little water to get it started. After blending, strain it. Nothing is better on a hot day, especially in Texas in August.

I was learning the importance of cleansing the body of built-up debris (petrified poop) and toxins in the tissue walls. Because of the increase in my elimination, I went in to have colonics once a week for the first eighteen months. Receiving a colonic is very up close and personal; it is important to find a colonic therapist with whom you feel comfortable. Fortunately, my first colonic therapist knew exactly what she was doing and was very caring and gentle. (Once again I want to stress that if you don't like the person, it's important to find someone else. This is your body and you are already traumatized enough. Make it as easy on yourself as you can.)

Colonics are also referred to as high colonics because with a colonic, water gets higher into the colon for cleansing than it does with enemas. A thin speculum is inserted into your rectum, and warm water begins flowing into your colon. (Remember to breathe and relax so the water can go as high into the colon as possible.) Once you are filled to your capacity, the water is turned off and flows back out carrying with it any debris such as fecal matter, mucus, watermelon seeds, and any other undigested food. This procedure not only cleans out your colon but also exercises the colon, making it stronger. The elimination of petrified remains allows the body to function more effectively and heal more quickly.

I talk about this so easily now, but the first time I went in I was terrified of this procedure. "Excuse me, but you're going to do what with the speculum?" I knew that I couldn't do this without the help of a valium. I was at the point of hysteria. I was wanting the "quick fix" approach so that everything would be back to normal in my life, not that I really knew anymore what normal meant.

My mother anticipated my fear and had scheduled a colonic for herself so that I could see that this procedure could be survived. She even went first in an effort to comfort me. I appreciated her efforts, but it didn't make me feel any better. After the first few times I was able to remain calm. I learned that the more relaxed I was the more I released from my bowels. I became fascinated with the strange and interesting creatures that would float by in the little glass tube. I was amazed that this stuff came out of me! It gave a new definition to the idea of being "full of it."

Many people prefer coffee enemas, but for me, colonics made more sense. I never did like to drink coffee, and I sure wasn't going to put it up the other end. Fortunately, I began to understand the importance of thoroughly cleansing the colon. The cleaner the colon, the more the colon is able to process toxins from other tissues and organs, a condition which allows more toxins to be released for elimination.

It takes years of poor diet, thoughts, and abusive patterns, whether conscious or unconscious, to break the body down to that place we call *disease*. Just as it takes years to dirty the body, it takes time to clean the body. It requires patience.

I began to think of disease as dis-ease. I was becoming aware that the body and mind can get into a place of dis-ease through fears stored within the body. My body was no exception. Elimination cleared the way for illumination.

The Doc Reams program works by maintaining a balance of nutrients in the body. Testing that monitors the saliva and urine is used to determine which vitamins are necessary to create an internal environment with maximum healing potential. Along with a strict diet that is a combination of vegetarianism and macrobiotics, the Reams program teaches the importance of cleansing the body through the use of lemon water, distilled water, and colonics.

Mr. and Mrs. Fry became my teachers. At every visit, they stressed the importance of cleansing the body, which in turn cleanses the mind. By choosing to cleanse the body through the use of nutrition and colonics, I started a detoxification process. Once my body became aware that it was time to dump the dis-ease, I increased my colonics to prevent a back-up of petrified waste. They explained that once the body decides to release, it is important to continue to flush out the toxins as quickly as possible. Even though I had been trying to do this quickly, there were times that I was not fast enough. Usually I was going in for colonics once a week, but there were a few weeks when I went twice.

A month into the diet and after just two colonics, I was waiting for my mother to come and pick me up to take me to my next colonic appointment. I began having some cramping in the abdominal area. At first I just thought that my jeans might have been too tight, so I changed. Momma arrived early as always, and I got in the car and began telling her that I was having some cramping when the pain became much more severe. I found myself screaming in the car and asked her to just take me home because I didn't think I could handle the drive. Momma insisted that I stay at her house that night, and she gathered a few of my things, all the while suggesting that maybe I should see a doctor. I refused and explained that I knew that my body was just releasing highly toxic waste (which it was). Nonetheless, the pain became extremely severe, my temperature began to rise, and I began vomiting. I couldn't sleep, and I was moaning and crying in pain. For two days I experienced continuous waves of nausea and pain – it was like a nightmare that wouldn't end. My mother sat beside my bed and read to me and told me to listen to the story she was reading. The only relief I had was during brief moments when I got lost in the story and didn't think of the pain. I refused medications of any kind.

Finally, my stepfather took my urine samples to Mr. and Mrs. Fry, so they could monitor my situation. In the evening, he called and said the tests revealed that I was on the verge of kidney failure. My mother and grandfather, Pap, immediately told me that I was going to the hospital, and they carefully loaded me into my Pap's camper van, wrapped in a warm, cozy blanket. The familiar sight of Parkland Hospital came into view as Pap pulled into Emergency. Terrified, with tears in his eyes, Pap took my hand and told me, "You've got to hold on. Fight. Be Strong." I was too weak to walk so an emergency assistant brought a wheelchair out to me.

My body was like an old rag doll; I was completely listless, at the mercy of God and the doctors. The waiting went on forever. Sometimes it seemed as if I were just an observer; at other times I was completely consumed by vomiting and screams of pains. Finally, someone came and took me into the examining room for X-rays. As the X-ray technician was setting me up for the X-ray, he asked me if I'd like to go on a date with him when I got to feeling better. How strange and odd – here I was green and puking, and this guy wants a date! The emergency room doctor prescribed some suppositories to stop the vomiting and sent me home. Morning was rapidly approaching as we left the hospital.

When we got back to my mother's house, Pap carried me

upstairs and put me to bed. My mother picked up the book and continued reading to me from the same story. My entire body hurt and I just lay there moaning in pain, but I started to get a glimpse of some relief as I fell off to sleep to the sound of her voice. When I woke up the pain was gone, but there was a stench. My entire body and gown were wet, and I was covered from the waist down with light brown fecal matter. I was so embarrassed. Sometime during the wee hours of the morning my body had decided to eliminate what smelled like radioactive waste. When my mother heard my crying, she got up.

"Momma, I'm so sorry."

"It's okay, Bethie, let's get you in the shower first." She helped me into the shower and got me washed and into a clean gown. Next, the mattress was dragged out onto the deck just down the hall. The mattress was washed, sterilized and left to air and dry. One more crisis had passed. I had also experienced my first healing crisis. This was exciting! I was alive, and my body was responding more quickly to the demand of healing. I knew that I was at a turning point.

When my healing crisis first began I thought, *oh no, I'm getting worse*, but instead, I learned first-hand that my body had to purge the illness. I had always thought that the body became sick because it was breaking down, and not for the purpose of cleaning house.

Chapter 5

Nothing More Than Today

Nothing in Life is to be feared.
It is only to be understood.
—Madame Curie

Two months before this whole saga began, James and I had moved into a new apartment; now I was living with a diagnosis of fourth-stage lymphoma, my boyfriend was gone, and I was unemployed. I moved into my mother's house. I remember going down to the apartment office to tell the manager I was moving. She told me that the company would sue me for the remainder of the lease. I shrugged my shoulders with indifference and said, "I've just been diagnosed with cancer and have been told that I'll probably be dead in six months, and I have no money. Go ahead and sue me." The woman softened her tone, and I never heard from the apartment complex again.

Even though I had begun a nutritional program to heal my body, my mind and spirit were wounded. I had thought I'd live forever – that this sort of thing happened only to other people, not me, but here I was among the statistics. I felt so totally alone and sad. Each day was filled with uncertainty. I had to do something about my mind because I continued to fall into waves of depression.

I asked, "Where do I start, God?"

The answer came, "Beth, just start with one thing at a

time, no matter how small it may seem."

Okay, first I must reconsider what the word CANCER means. The very mention of CANCER was enough to kill some people. They would just fall over and die. I wasn't going to do that.

Somewhere in the depths of my soul I knew that there was nothing that could not be solved or healed, and that, therefore, nothing was impossible. Where was this information coming from? I didn't know. I decided to look at my cancer experience as if I had a cold and I knew that a cold was known to be curable. I also decided to clearly state my diagnosis. I started saying that I had been diagnosed with fourth-stage poorly differentiated small-cell lymphoma. When I hear people say, "I have cancer," I respond by asking them what type of cancer they've been diagnosed with. I don't believe cancer should be lumped into one big "black cloud" category. I knew this wasn't about the word, cancer, but about my entire way of thinking.

I was beginning the process of being my own physician, scientist, researcher, and lab rat and the healer of my soul. I had to acquire as much knowledge as I possibly could; I became a vacuum for holistic knowledge (a more complete and whole solution). I had a purpose in life, and my adrenaline gained in speed as it pumped through my veins. I told myself that I had to take this experience and do with it the very best I could and to prove that I could turn it around. As I began feeling this new-found energy and enthusiasm, depression became like a distant cousin.

I began being drawn to colors and noticed how I felt wearing different shades and colors. Violets and purples were my choice. After I began working with color on my own, I started to read about the importance of color in treatment and therapy. My research revealed that the colors in the violet family stimulate the process of purification of the blood, reduce inflammations, stimulate the growth of white blood cells, maintain the potassium-sodium balance of the body, lower blood pressure and much more! This was fascinating to me. Here on my own I had chosen colors that I later found out actually improved my blood.

One day I woke up and my entire body, from my face to my feet, was very swollen. I didn't have a clue as to why, but I had read that turquoise would reduce swelling. This was definitely an experiment in motion, so I began putting on everything I had that was turquoise until my whole body except for my face was covered. I had on turquoise underwear, tights, turtle neck, ski cap, and socks. I went back to bed and just lay there and absorbed the color into my body while meditating. Within fifteen minutes the swelling was gone, and I was relaxed. It was absolutely amazing that something so light-hearted, so much fun, and so informative was working. I knew also that if I hadn't have taken action, I wouldn't have seen results. This was a major realization. Angels, spirit guides, strangers, or my own intuition directed and offered me vast sums of knowledge and information, but if I didn't take action, nothing was going to happen.

Chapter 6

Gratitude For the Little Things

Patience is the companion of wisdom
–St. Augustine

This entire program was like synchronized, enlightened chaos. My daily mediation seemed to be "Chop wood, carry water." Whether I was walking or eating, everything I did on a daily basis seemed in some way part of my program. Every day my mother and I would walk a couple of miles. I needed some kind of exercise daily to increase circulation and boost the oxygen level in my blood stream. It didn't matter what the weather was like, Momma and I were out walking. She did everything with me – the new eating habits, the walks, the colonics, etc. – because she wanted to let me know that I was not alone on this journey. In many ways I was alone, but I was very grateful and honored that my mother chose to keep time with my rhythm. She was the heartbeat that kept everything together until I could do it on my own.

I had been recovering for close to a year at my mother's house. By this time my health was becoming stronger with each day, and I was feeling the need to gain some autonomy. My grandparents offered me a room in their house which was like a small studio apartment, so I moved in. Their home was only a few miles from my mother's and looked out onto Lake Grapevine. My room had a private entrance and a view over both the lake and the swimming pool. My grandfather and I had moved their furniture out and had moved my furniture in so it felt more like my place.

Yes, I'd made a lot of changes by now. Let's see. . . . I had gone from eating meat three times a day, doing drugs and drinking, to becoming a vegetarian who juiced my fruits and vegetables. Colonics, fasts, parasite cleanses, liver and gall bladder flushes (see summary), vitamins, herbs, color work and exercise had all become part of my daily routine. What next? I knew there was always more to learn.

So I continued reading to feed my soul and to explore other means to improve my health. My outlook on life became very focused and serious even though I used humor to get through the tough moments. My life was changing, and with each day I was allowing my body, mind and spirit to be molded by God. Not the God who wears a white robe, sits on His throne and looks like Charlton Heston, but a God who represents an energy and connection between and within all of us. This decision of taking God off His throne took me to new heights.

My reading lead me to a story about a man named Edgar Cayce. I became fascinated with his development along the path of illumination, as well as with the many people he helped. Through my studies of Edgar Cayce and the Association for Research and Enlightenment, (A.R.E.), I began to use the castor oil packs he so often mentioned for cleansing. Castor oil packs were a suggested treatment in cleansing the lymph system and the body in general. Castor oil, according to ancient times, meant oil from the palm of Christ. The plant is called palma Christi.

Okay, I thought, *I'll experiment.* I wrote down the items I needed and laid them out. I needed castor oil, a piece of white flannel, a heating pad, a plastic bag, and a towel. Next, I heated the castor oil and then soaked the flannel in the oil. After the flannel had been soaked in the oil, I placed it over my chest or upper body because the "spaghetti bowl" for the lymphatic system is under the sternum or breast-plate area. The lymphatic system has both deep and superficial vessels. The deeper vessels often travel with the deeper arteries and nerves, which are more concentrated under and around the sternum. Because of the messiness of the oil, I needed to place the plastic bag over the flannel before I placed the heating pad on top. The towel was to wipe my hands with, and because of the need to stay still for a few hours I also learned to have the phone, a book, food, water, and maybe a good movie close at hand. According to Edgar Cayce's work, these packs needed to be done nightly for one to two months. I committed to one month, but after that I got tired of the constant cleanup.

I could actually feel a definite improvement in my overall health while I used the castor oil packs, but the mess always made me hesitate. Sometimes now I might use them for a night or two, but it's only when I'm desperate. Probably if I would do it when the first sign of some sort of cold sets in, I could be done with the cold before it starts. But when every moment of every day is spent thinking about the next step of what you need to do for improving your health, it's sometime nice to rebel and just say "No!"

During the first year following my diagnosis, I kept a weekly appointment with my chiropractor because I wanted to maintain the suppleness of my spine. I learned that the energy that flows up through the body needs to be free of obstructions. The spine carries vital fluids through it and protects the many nerves. If this structure is jammed in any way, the body will not have the necessary flow of energy. I felt that chiropractic was vital to my health and would keep me feeling strong and whole. From my neck to tailbone, my spine remained aligned. My chiropractic alignments also changed as I changed chiropractors so I could maintain a high quality of care, which later included cranial adjustments.

I was starting to sound like a doctor. I found myself always bouncing back and forth between being a doctor, scientist, patient, lab rat, and just trying to be a kid.

I was growing up, and this was reflected by my mind becoming increasingly healthier. I had begun reading and studying many areas to lift me both mentally and spiritually. This reading included the life and works of Edgar Cayce, which I've already mentioned, Emmet Fox's *Sermon on the Mount*, Dan Millman's *The Way of the Peaceful Warrior*, and countless others. But no matter how much I was reading and focusing on healing myself, I needed to be with friends. Even though my friends of my past supported me in my decision, our lifestyles were different. I needed to make new and healthier friends.

One of my girlfriends was pregnant and her husband had left her, so we found mutual support and a stronger friendship in return. Tanya and I had known each other for many years and had gone off on a few wild adventures together, but now we both had changed for the better. She needed a Lamaze coach but wasn't sure about asking me since I was fighting to stay alive. When Tanya did ask me to be her Lamaze coach, I was delighted. I needed some mental diversion away from just me and my daily routine. This friendship proved very fortunate for me.

Tanya had a little dessert store called Frougerts in Dallas on lower Greenville. I'd go by and help her at the shop or just hang out and visit. She knew I was focusing to maintain my diet and new lifestyle, so she would make sure the restaurants where we ate served food I could eat. I found myself eating every time she ate, which was often. I was having a blast and putting on a little weight myself. We'd go to Lamaze classes and everywhere together, and the closer she got to her due date the more I stayed at her mother's house to be close to her.

I had just spent the last week at Tanya's house because it was getting close to her due date, so I decided to drive back out to Lake Grapevine. Tanya called me about nine in the evening and told me she thought she had begun labor, but she wasn't sure since she'd falsely labored on two earlier occasions. She told me not to worry and she'd call if it got worse. I had been in bed about thirty minutes when the phone rang. It was Tanya's mother, Beth, calling to tell me that Tanya had panicked and gone to the hospital and that her husband had shown up. I threw on my clothes and jumped in the car. It took me forty-five minutes to get from Lake Grapevine to Baylor Hospital in Dallas. I was flying, and the gods were on my side, because I never even had to stop at a red light.

I found so much strength in helping her during her hours of need. The only break I took was when Tanya's mom relieved me long enough so I could take a forty-minute nap the following day. Twenty-one hours later Katy was born. I was excited! Participating in the birthing process was wonderful. Katy came out beautiful and pumping her muscles. Nine pounds and eleven ounces. I found myself outside the nursery window telling strangers, "Yea, that's my kid; isn't she just beautiful?" Some people probably thought I was crazy but it didn't matter. What I realized through this experience was that it was important for me in my life to always help other people.

Beth and I left the hospital, and she took me to dinner. It was after dinner that I realized how tired I was. When I returned to her house I fell asleep for twelve hours.

It was a wonderful and love-filled experience to see a life being born. This experience strengthened my outlook on becoming healthier and even more positive. Any thoughts about whether my life would be taken from me or not seemed distant and strange. I planted my feet in the ground and made my stand; I was keeping my earth suit and staying for a while. By gosh, I had work to do on this planet! I wasn't sure what it was yet, but it would come to me.

Chapter 7
The Power of Healing

Don't be afraid to go out on a limb.
That's where the fruit is.
—Anonymous

It's one thing when a small child is afraid of the dark, but it's
another thing when a grown man is afraid of the light.
—Source Unknown

With my renewed sense of self and the help of my angels, I was introduced to Reiki, a form of energy healing, by a newfound friend. Ann and I found support and encouragement from each other because we both wanted to be healthier. When she told me about Reiki, I thought..."*Energy healing, Reiki..., something invisible. Okay, I'm going to take a leap of faith.*" Another new ingredient was added to my list of healing modalities.

"Rei" means spiritually guided and "Ki" means light-force energy. This ancient way of healing by attuning or aligning the energy centers excited me. This wasn't part of academia or lessons in barrel racing. From what I understood, Reiki had been rediscovered when some old manuscripts had been unearthed and then later translated in the mid-1800's. I found Reiki to be very rewarding in gaining personal strength and faith in the unknown. When I thought of the invisible energies, I realized that they're not unknown, but simply have not been taught because of so many eons of being hidden. I learned that we are energy and that all illness begins in the energy field first before manifesting itself in the physical and emotional bodies.

This energy healing made sense to me. I would be learning to understand the opening up or redirecting of pathways for the energy that naturally flows throughout all life. I could apply this energy to both myself and to other people by simply allowing the concentrated energy to be guided through my hands. Reiki also flowed through my eyes and feet. The healing universal energy came through me and out my hands and into the person or animal I was working on, and in turn I, too, received energy. All of these new ideas and concepts with diet, energy, and color resonated with my spirit. I was proving their effectiveness for myself through my own inner knowing and experiences, and I didn't need validation from conventional sources.

For years I have continued to use Reiki and other healing energies on myself, my animals, and other people. By using the healing forces, I have been able to cope with life's challenges better and open myself to greater creativity and clearer expressions or thoughts.

Chapter 8

Cinderella

We turn, not older with years, but newer every day.
−Emily Dickinson

Prepare your mind to receive the best life has to offer.
−Ernest Holmes

I was coming up on April 21, 1984, the one-year mark of my diagnosis, and I was doing fantastic. I felt alive and in control! The lifestyle that had started out as foreign to me now seemed very familiar and somehow I felt as if my body and soul were also more integrated because of the healthier changes that I had made. My spirit strengthened because of my entire routine was like a daily moving mediation of being focused only on today, the present moment.

For this milestone Momma wanted to honor and recognize the changes in me and had planned a very elaborate celebration, which she was able to splurge on because she had just sold her house. She wouldn't tell me what she had planned, but only that it started with shopping. She took me to an exclusive boutique and told me to pick out the most beautiful dress and shoes I could find. I picked out a dress of peach chiffon, with a dropped waistline, spaghetti straps and a peach chiffon jacket that was sewn into the dropped waist. The jacket decorated with embroidered leaves and flowers. My shoes were light pecan-colored satin with an ankle strap and open toes. Across the toes sat three rhinestones. My shoes were actually a half-size too big, but they were the last pair, and I wanted them.

I still didn't know what all of this was for, and the excitement was mounting. The next morning I was told that I had a hair appointment. My hair was done in curls on top of my head and curls around my neck with a salmon-colored rose placed in my hair. A dozen salmon roses had been delivered in the morning. I felt like I was Cinderella as I stood in front of the mirror in my new dress, shoes, and hairdo. Next came a chauffeured 1936 two-tone burgundy and white Rolls Royce. The limousine company told us that they had purchased the Rolls Royce from Marilyn Monroe's estate. They had placed a red rose in a silver and glass vase on the inside panel of the door. The chauffeur opened the door, and I stepped inside my elegant coach. My mother said that I could do anything I wanted until midnight. I simply wanted to drive around and enjoy the ride.

I found it amazing that people would wave and honk their horns, and I would wave and smile at them. They had no idea who I was but knew that I must be someone important. Next we were off to Turtle Creek to meet a photographer and begin the most dazzling of photo shoots. Momma and I had pictures done together as well as separately. As soon as the photo shoot began, a crowd started gathering around us. They didn't know who we were but thought that this must be for a magazine. The hushed whispers drifted through the air leaving a trail of tales of models and celebrities or of an heiress of a great fortune! After the photo shoot the chauffeur opened the door and drove us to The Mansion, an elegant, five-star restaurant, for dinner. As my Rolls for the day pulled up to the front drive, the valet opened my door and escorted me to the restaurant.

Before I placed my order I had already called the Frys and asked if a little meat or wine would hurt since it was just this once. I promised that this was only a momentary change from my hard-earned new habits. They assured me that this was okay. My dinner began with escargot followed by a main course of rack of lamb with a medley of vegetables. I had a glass of wine with dinner and then finished the evening with a Grand Marnier soufflé. I can't say that there was much conversation, just a few words here and there. I had learned to be present in my life, and this moment vibrated with quiet elegance.

When we got up to leave, the valet was notified of our departure, and I could see him with the most vigorous of arm motions signaling my driver that I was ready. As I sat waiting for my Rolls, the manager of the restaurant introduced himself to me and wanted to be sure that everything had been to my satisfaction. He didn't know who I was, but he was sure I must be a VIP of some kind.

As the chauffeur drove us back, I was beginning to fade just as the sun had fallen from sight. My midnight came around 11:30 p.m., and the beautiful two-tone burgundy and white chauffeur-driven Rolls Royce turned into a Chevrolet. My day had been filled with abundant love and adventure, and I slept very well that night and on into the late morning. It had been a day of fairy tales, and I was Cinderella.

Chapter 9

Power of Thoughts

You never can tell what a thought will do
In bringing you hate or love –
For thoughts are things, and their airy wings
Are swifter than carrier doves.
They follow the law of the Universe
Each thing creates its kind.
And they speed o'er the track to bring you back
Whatever went out from your mind.
—Ella Wheeler Wilcox

The Chinese word for crisis is written with two brush strokes.
The first is for danger and the second for opportunity.
—Anonymous, *Confusion Is A State Of Grace*

A few months after my day of being Cinderella, I decided it was time to go back to Parkland and have my blood tested. I wanted to make sure that everything was clear. I needed some confirmation in writing that everything was normal. A friend of my sister's was a doctor involved with research in the oncology department. She promised that he was a caring and nice man, and she had spent some time with him discussing me and my situation. I tentatively decided that somehow he could be trusted and that I would see him. His name was Dr. Daniel Flynn, and he was very polite. He seemed genuinely fascinated with what I was doing. He didn't understand my natural regimen, but he said to continue with the program.

His office was in a building between the hospital and a building that did animal testing. My stomach would get squeamish everytime I walked by the place where they did the animal testing. The first time I met with Dr. Flynn, I told him that he was to put me in an examining room immediately because I would not wait. I always did this with a smile and a sense of humor, but I was very serious. I had spent too much time with doctors who seemed to forget that they were working for me. He knew to take me seriously because he had heard stories about me which had made the rounds. He would tell the nurses to put me in a room with only one exit, so I couldn't sneak out the back. The lab technician would practically carry my vials of blood on a pillow to the lab because I told him if he dropped it, he wouldn't get any more. Dr. Flynn always took good care of me.

Every day I checked myself for any type of swelling or tumor. I called them knots. One particular day I had gone with my mother as she took my sister, Becky, to pick out a kitten. While Becky was playing with the litter of Himalayan kittens, I began feeling around my body for swellings. I did this unconsciously, out of habit, but today there was a little bit of anxiety. I didn't know what the nervousness was about until I felt it, a knot, on my back. I somehow knew immediately that it was malignant.

My mom called Dr. Flynn and arranged to get me in quickly. Scared, I told Dr. Flynn that I had found a knot on my back. He ordered a biopsy. I knew that the knot was small and the biopsy of it alone would probably remove almost all of it. There was a young doctor to whom he referred me; he said that she would perform the procedure in her office. I don't remember her name, but she was very pleasant. The biopsy was performed, and within a few days the results came back. Malignant. All I wanted was for the tumor to be cut out. I didn't want it in my body. One week later that same doctor removed the remainder of the tumor. Both Dr. Flynn and this other doctor wanted me to follow up with radiation, but I refused. I was just glad that the tumor was gone, but I also knew that I couldn't keep having them cut tumors out each time one popped up. I knew that the tumor might have formed as part of the natural healing process that the lymphatic system performs to collect and filter out toxins from the body, but I was afraid not to cut it out for fear of it spreading.

Fears are like fires; they can destroy and spread rapidly. Sometimes we get so caught up in tunnel vision that we fail to see the larger picture. I tried to remember that in seeing the larger scheme of things I needed to step back and breathe and let the smoke clear as I let go of my fears.

Chapter 10

Amongst the Living

All that I give, I give to Myself.
—A Course In Miracles

Effort only releases its reward after a person refuses to quit.
—Napoleon Hill

Roughly two years into my program I thought my sanity was coming back. *Life was definitely looking up. I'm realizing that I'd fought for my life, relationships, financial stability, old thought patterns, and my soul. I had survived when no one thought that I would. I thought this was one of those life-altering experiences. My mind was strong and I had proven that a strict nutritional program can reverse a life-threatening illness.*

I had enrolled in a few classes at the community college and was enjoying them. I had also started a new job, which was perfect because the hours were few, the pay was good, and it was low stress. I shined shoes in a hotel. My upper body was having the greatest workout and was getting stronger in the process. Between this job and the exercise I got in my jazz dance class at school, I was getting into the best shape of my life.

One weekend the woman I was working for asked if I would want to work a Cattleman's convention. It sounded like fun. I don't think I ever worked harder! Every time I looked up I had cowboys lined up ten deep behind me. In three hours I had shined more boots than you could possibly imagine. I shined until my arms ached and the convention concluded.

Before long, I had my own shoeshine business. I had contracts with a hotel, a country-western bar, and three office buildings, and I had one of my sisters working for me part-time. In addition, I was also selling estate jewelry for a woman in Dallas, Cathy Camplen. Cathy had taken me under her wing. One of her sons had been born on the same month, day and year that I was born, and his daughter had lived through a cancer experience at a very early age. She called me her child and considered me his twin. Cathy, with her antiques, taught me a lot about jewelry and people and about having fun. A bonus was being able to play with all the beautiful pieces of jewelry.

Over and over, I was finding out that people everywhere were all so willing to help me. And in some way I felt like I was giving back to each of them. I was realizing that all we have to do is ask, and we will receive; but learning to receive is not something that we are necessarily taught or are comfortable with.

Chapter 11

Dreams

The invariable mark of wisdom is to see the miraculous in the common.
—Ralph Waldo Emerson

As more and more time passed, I began to gather more pieces or ingredients together that gave me what I needed to learn about healing. The interesting thing that I was finding out was that everything is interconnected, so you need to consider all aspects of your self: body, mind and spirit. In school I had enrolled in a dream psychology class. This class was just the beginning for me. I was fascinated with dreams and did additional reading outside of my required reading for the class. As I kept my dream journal, I began to look back on dreams that I had had prior to my diagnosis. I was finding such major connections and information in retrospect that, had I known then what I was learning now, I believe I could have made earlier corrections in my health and prevented much of my disease. These dreams had been trying to warn me of the danger within, but I did not know what they meant at the time. However, I sure got that "ah ha" feeling now.

Dream 1: This dream had been recurring for more than a year prior to diagnosis. It was always dark, so dark it was hard to see. In the earlier versions of the dream I was being chased relentlessly by a dark figure. I never saw what it looked like. I came to a wall that had different doors within an arch-way, but all the doors that I would open and go inside to hide would always have another door that would not open. Then, in later dreams, the pace was much faster and the figure was on a motorcycle. I ran so fast, but once again I came to that same arched doorway. It looked like it would lead to a courtyard and to safety, but there was another door inside that door. I hid between the two doors, hoping the motorcycle would not catch me, and at the same time I knew that the only way out was back through the door that I had just entered.

I would always wake up before I opened the door, but when I awoke I would be terrified, in a cold sweat with clutched fists. I believe that this was death trying to catch me, and it almost did.

Dream 2: This dream continued to recur for almost the same length of time as the first one. Someone I knew had been taken prisoner and placed in a cage which was in a dungeon of hell. The dungeon held many captive souls. Some cells were just suspended from the ceiling while others where terraced. Everything was red and orange in color, but the entire environment looked like ravished, decaying flesh. Some of the people were dead, and others were dying. I knew if I could get to just one, my friend, that everything would be all right, but I had to arrange for this escape. The tortured, dying souls were everywhere; there was only one shot at success. In later dreams of this escape, there were a couple of other people who were able to help me rescue one soul, but I always woke up while looking for safety.

These dreams were always so vivid and frightening. If only I had known what my dreams had meant at the time. I tried to tell myself it didn't matter that I hadn't known, but I kept thinking it did matter because knowing could have changed the course of events in my life. But, now, I had learned that just by acknowledging the dreams, I was telling my subconscious that I was listening and that the meanings would come later, which, of course, they did.

I wish that dream interpretation would be a required course in school, beginning with grade school. I believe the people on this planet would be much more conscious if we had understanding of our dreams.

I found that I was a natural at understanding my dreams, and I found myself helping others interpret their dreams. I continued to study and read about dreams, and in many ways I believe that we are more asleep when we're awake than when we're asleep. I pay attention to all my dreams now. I know when the dreams just seem to be rehashing some of the day's dilemmas or when they are offering me a message of hope, encouragement, or a warning of what is to come.

One of my angelic helpers was a big black man with short hair. He only came to me in my dreams. Most of the time he would be holding my hand and guiding me through ice, snow, or water, and sometimes he would carry me. I was always a small child, never an adult. He would never talk, but he didn't have to because we understood each other. I knew that he would keep me safe.

Chapter 12

The Catacombs of My Mind

Untwisting all the chains that tie the hidden soul of harmony
—John Milton

It was 1986. Three years had passed since my diagnosis, and I was in my second year of school. I was shining shoes at the night club one evening, and one of my customers, Jerry, was saying he was fed up with women and was moving to Reno. He had lived there for a few years growing up and really liked it. I just listened. All of my customers had their stories, and I was like the bartender or hairdresser that knew more about them than their spouses did.

By this time I was doing numerology and intuitive readings for friends and family members. Jerry had heard that I did numerology charts and asked if I would help him because he needed to make this move soon and wanted it to be successful for him. Somehow that conversation grew, and we started to become friends. And then, in the blink of an eye, we were in love. In less than two months we were married, and I was moving to Reno, Nevada. I had been to Reno once before, but only for a couple of days. I had been ready to move out of Dallas for quite some time. My personal plans had been to move to Austin, Texas, but Reno sounded like fun and would do.

Shortly before Jerry and I got married, I began having tumultuous dreams again, but this time they had to do with my mother turning against me. She was fighting with me and another person. At first I couldn't figure the dreams out.

My mother wouldn't turn against me. Not me. She loved me.

Well, once my mother realized that Jerry and I were getting married and that I was going to be moving to Nevada with him, I could sense a developing mood and pressure from her and some of my other family members. She would make comments that we were moving too fast and that she didn't trust him. Despite her mistrust, I maintained my decision to marry and move to Nevada with Jerry.

I know that my mother tried really hard to maintain composure, but while she was helping me pack, she went ballistic. Next thing I knew she had called her husband over and asked him to bring his gun. She was going to stay until Jerry came and got his things out of my apartment. I felt out of control. My mother wouldn't listen to anything I said, and, at that point, I wouldn't listen to her either. All I could do was to ask Jerry to get his things and to tell him I would talk to my mother and try to get her to calm down. I definitely didn't want anyone shot. It was a mess. He called me, crying, asking me what was going on and, all the while, my mother was standing there telling me to tell him that I would never see him again. I kept trying to get my mother to understand that I would be okay and that I would write and stay in touch. She didn't hear a word I said; she was hysterical. She couldn't believe that I would just decide to fall in love and move. She believed I was being rash and making a mistake. I explained to her that I knew what I was doing and that I deserved to have love. Once again my dreams were right.

I finally got some kind of control back, or so I thought. I demanded that my mother leave and allow me my space. After she left, I took a deep breath and called Jerry. When he arrived, he asked where I had parked my car. I told him that it should be out front, but it wasn't. My mother had her name on everything I owned from my car to my bank accounts, and she even had a key to my apartment. By the next morning my mother had emptied out my safety deposit box, in addition to having stolen my car. Luckily, I made it to one bank before she got there. Jerry changed the locks on the door. My world as I knew it had been shattered. My mother had been my best friend and more to me, and now I wasn't sure who she was.

On February 1, 1987, two weeks after the blowup, Jerry and I quietly married. His brother and a good friend of mine served as witnesses. We found a minister who provided a lovely ceremony in his home, and then Jerry's brother took us out for dinner. There was no honeymoon because we would be leaving for Reno in a few days, and there was plenty of packing left to do.

Just a day or so after the wedding and a few days prior to our exodus, my mother wrote me a seven-page letter telling me how awful my husband was and how I did not know the truth. She accused him of being a murderer. When she had gone nuts at my house earlier, she had found a rusty chef's knife, and she believed that the rust was blood. Even though I had told her that he was a chef, she wouldn't listen. Her written tale continued to carve out a story of a horrible, painful death I would experience, and she told me that I needed to face up to the facts. I was devastated. I didn't know how she could do this to me. We had been so close.

Everything seemed to be moving so fast. I was fighting on a daily basis to keep from having a nervous breakdown. I felt my mother, the one person who I thought would never do anything to hurt me, had tried to destroy me. I tried to find some understanding, but none came. All the spiritual insight I had gained seemed gone.

Jerry and I hooked up the U-Haul trailer behind our car. As we drove out of Dallas, the clouds opened and with the opening came a deluge. As the rain came in sheets, we cried uncontrollably. The earth seemed to share in our pain, and we felt all we had was each other.

Life didn't seem quite so sad and forlorn once we got out of Texas. The drive was long, but luckily I had other family along the way who hadn't blacklisted me. Our stops were a welcome, refreshing, and relaxing change from those last hellish days in Dallas. As we drove through the Sierra Nevada mountain passes, the scenery was breathtaking. The land started to change radically from piney mountain forests to high-desert mountains as we arrived in Reno. The mountains, both forest and desert, were beautiful, yet all the houses were brown and looked just alike. I was realizing that each city had its own personality and Reno was no exception. Even though we were able to relax some, we were exhausted by the time we arrived in Reno.

We stayed with Jerry's ex-wife and her husband. At first I was apprehensive about staying with Leslie, but she was very gracious. Jerry and Leslie had been divorced for a long time and were on good terms. They shared a daughter together whom his parents were raising.

The house was full between the four of us and the combined five cats. At night, our five cats sounded more like elephants as they ran through the house. The cats had established a hierarchy. My older cat, Sylvester, had taken the position of leader of the pack and protected my younger cat, Baby Girl. I enjoyed the diversion of their universe; it seemed simpler than ours.

Within a couple of weeks of our arrival, we both had jobs, and we had found a place to live, so we began to see our new life together as positive, and we were growing closer. Jerry had taken a job as a cook and was going to dealer's school. I was working as a dealer in the Eldorado Hotel & Casino in Reno to help us get on our feet. I hadn't been a dealer before I moved to Reno, but there are advantages to being a pretty woman with a Southern drawl. I simply walked in and applied for a position as a dealer. The personnel office said, "But you don't deal." I told them that's what I wanted to do, so they hired me and put me through their in-house training program. After Jerry completed his dealer's school, he got into gaming as well. We were starting to do pretty well financially. We established credit, got a listed phone number, and felt like respectable folks.

In the beginning I had thought working as a dealer would somehow be glamorous. Wrong. I had become aware of my body declining and losing energy, which I attributed to the smoke-filled casino. The smoke was hard on me. By the time I got off work, I'd feel like a walking cigarette. I'd tell people, "I don't need to smoke; I work in a casino." The filtration system was zip to none.

I would get so angry when people blew their smoke in my face. And if they came up with a cigar, I would begin to turn green; if they asked if the smoke bothered me, I had a sarcastic response. I didn't care if they sat at my table or not. I remember one man who came to sit at my game and was smoking. Every time he'd blow the smoke in my face, I'd blow it back. The funny part was that he was wearing a toupee, and every time I blew, the toupee would ripple up. He would look up and mumble something about a draft. The whole table was laughing hysterically, and he couldn't figure out what was so funny. He didn't know that I was the draft.

On top of the smoke, I had been fighting depression and anger since receiving my mother's last letter in Dallas. I couldn't believe that she would do this to me. I thought our relationship had been special, and I was devastated. It felt like my body had begun to fall apart almost as soon as she spoke the words of my death. I would read the letter over and over in shock and horror. My posture had even changed, and I was looking more like someone with a curved spine. In actuality, my spine was curving. It was because of her letter that I began learning to look at illness from a different approach. I began to see and understand the energy connections that were plugged into me at birth. As I explored these energies intuitively, I found beliefs that had been branded into my soul for this human experience. I had both the cultural collective consciousness of the cancer experience, and I had beliefs that I needed to suffer to be worthy, along with unexpressed anger and fear. Doctors and scientists say that many diseases are predetermined and are passed down through the generations because of genetics and DNA, but I questioned this theory. I feel beliefs are passed first through thought transference, and that it is these beliefs that then create the diseases or illnesses.

One night I couldn't take another minute of the pain of my mother's words, so Jerry and I went outside to burn her letter. I gave thanks to the heavens that these words of anger, pain, and dying would be released from me. Each page was placed in a casserole dish and burnt under the starry Nevada night sky. As the letter burned, I felt a healing process beginning. This ritual seemed to help, and I began to feel better for a little while. What I didn't know was that to reclaim myself was to simultaneously enter into a valley of both death and light.

Her words had total mental power over my own mind, "You don't know the truth, you will die a horrible, painful death." "You don't know the truth, you'll never escape the disease. . . ." Over and over I could hear those words. And each day I hoped that Momma would call and say, "I love you, Bethie; will you forgive me? "

At first the decline seemed to be gradual, but then it began to pick up momentum. Because of the deterioration of my posture, I went in for weekly chiropractic manipulations. Dr. Weis, my chiropractor, also suggested that I have special inserts made for my shoes because my arches were falling. Structurally, my body was collapsing. I found it interesting that my mother had been my main support early in my healing and now that she was gone, my skeletal structure was going, too.

If we were to stop and think about the similarities between our thoughts and what goes on physically, we could use the knowledge to change our lives before any further deterioration happens. Our bodies respond to our thoughts, and our energy fields respond first, before our bodies. In other words, when I received the letter, I felt devastated. I had allowed her words to disempower me. The change showed up in my energy field first. I had even stated that I couldn't *stand* the pain anymore and that my mother had been my main support. After my mother's letter came, my inability to stand physically followed. It was only natural at this juncture that my arches fell and my spine begin to curve. The connections were endless. *The inner guidance within me and my own body is always trying to tell me what was going on, but did I listen?* I was trying, but at the same time I wasn't listening.

Now my impairment was picking up speed. I had been working in the casino for six months, and I found myself getting tired more and more easily and coming down with one "bug" after another. It seemed like I always had a runny nose. Jerry was frequently nursing me back to health. He was always supportive and comforting to me. After about eight months, I started noticing enlarged glands that did not recede. "Oh, my God," I thought, "I don't know what to do." I would go into the bathroom or bedroom, someplace where Jerry couldn't see or hear me, and cry and scream. How could this happen? I was newly married and in love! I did not want to die! Even though I tried to hide, Jerry knew that

I was upset. He had known before we got married what I had already gone through. One day I said, "Jerry, the tumors have come back. I don't want to die, but I'm scared."

Falling to my knees, I'd scream at God, "I will not die and if you want me, you will have to come down and take me because I refuse to die!" I had incredible will and my motivation for survival began to roll at a high rate of speed; I would do anything to live. The one thing I didn't realize was that I had taken my mother's words as truth. A small child does not want to disappoint a parent. The small child in me had sealed her words in the flame as her letter burnt through me.

I knew that I had incredible will power, but I had allowed the limitation, represented by my mother's words, to occupy space within my mind, locking itself in my core as truth. It didn't matter how much I knew nutritionally or mentally; I could still hear my mother's words, "You don't know the truth, you will die a horrible, painful death, you will never escape the disease." These words haunted my memory no matter how much I demanded them to leave. I wanted to pick up the phone and scream at my mother and tell her how much I hated her and how I blamed her for what was happening to me. But I knew that I was responsible for allowing her thoughts to have power over me.

"Okay, now, full-tilt survivor mode. This can be done." I began walking five miles a day to increase the oxygen flow. I'd get up at 5:00 a.m. and walk, whether there was snow or not. Next, I cleaned up my diet again. No more junk food, even if it pretended to be healthy.

In November, 1988, I found out that laetrile was legal in Nevada, and I began going to a clinic and having laetrile and vitamin injections. I would go in before work and sit for two or three hours while the laetrile and vitamins would drip into my veins. Then I would go to the casino to work an eight-hour shift. The little bit of energy I did have was not enough to maintain or replenish my reserve. It didn't matter that I knew all the right things to do or that I had the will power and focus to do every last detail, because I had already disempowered myself with my mother's words.

As the days passed, I continued to get worse. Tumors were appearing everywhere – in my neck, armpits, joints and groin – and they were growing. I stopped even keeping count because there were too many. Towards the end of the laetrile injections my husband and my nurse who was giving me the IV's were saying that I needed to consider seeing an oncologist. Even my father in El Paso, whom I spoke to only infrequently, was advising me to see "a real doctor." On top of this, I was dreaming at night about not being able to finish school. I was told, "School is still in session, and it's time for your doctorate degree." I kept telling the teacher that I had already taken this class and graduated, and I asked why I was being brought back to do the same thing again. The teacher said that I hadn't learned "it" and I needed to do "it" again, but once I completed the course, "You will be truly graduated." She continued saying that I had agreed to this contract before I entered my earth suit on this planet. I had thought that through all the pain and growing of the past years the school part of my life had ended. Wrong! I really wanted my owner's manual now.

Chapter 13

Chemotherapy

When the heart weeps for what it has lost,
the soul laughs for what it has found.
—Sufi aphorism

The nurse from the laetrile clinic had referred me to Dr. James Forsythe, whom she recommended because of his open-mindedness. She had worked with him many years earlier while she was in school. I said I'd think about it, and I gave myself permission to take a day or two to process my thoughts and feelings. After weighing the information, I decided to at least go and listen to what the man had to say. I had come to the conclusion that I should not limit my views of the medical field as I had seen the medical field and the alternative field do to each other. Besides, I was beginning to realize that the woman who ran the laetrile clinic seemed to be more interested in the income of the patients than of their well being. The treatments were costing me a small fortune.

My first visit with Dr. Forsythe seemed to be just what I needed to break this spell or curse I was under. Dr. Forsythe was extremely optimistic and told me that everything would be okay. He said that the other doctors had been wrong to say that I was going to die because no one knows. This statement alone brought me peace of mind and helped me begin the mental battle to regain my control. Dr. Forsythe also gave me credit and respect for the success I had achieved on my own; he considered my program to be of great value and thought that I should continue with the nutritional and spiritual work. He also wanted me to begin immediately on chemotherapy. The thought of losing my hair was devastating. I wasn't sure that I could deal with that loss. Once again, I told Jerry, Dr. Forsythe, and my father that I would need to take twenty-four hours to think this through.

Right before my first visit with Dr. Forsythe, I had begun to work the graveyard shift, 2 a.m. to 10 a.m., at the casino. That way I didn't have to take days off for my doctor's appointments or hospital testing. I went to the assistant shift supervisor and explained my situation, and he was very cooperative. I explained that I needed to maintain my full-time status so that my insurance would remain effective. At the beginning of my week-end, I would leave work and head over to Dr. Forsythe's office for chemo. This way I would have two to three days off to be totally sick and miserable, so when I returned to work, I would have improved to just feeling awful.

Before he administered the chemotherapy, Dr. Forsythe wanted a biopsy to ensure that the chemicals he used would treat the disease identified in my original diagnosis. I, too, wanted to make sure that whatever he mixed in his magic cauldron was the exact recipe I needed. I met with the surgeon and he arranged for my biopsy.

On the morning of the biopsy surgery, the surgeon called the hospital to say that he had an emergency and would be several hours late, so I put my clothes back on and went home. Arrangements were made to have the biopsy done two days later under local anesthesia in the emergency room. I refused to go under a general anesthesia since the biopsies were performed just under the surface of the skin, and a slice of skin was all that was taken. The diagnosis remained the same – poorly differentiated, small-cell lymphoma. Chemotherapy began on April 13, 1989, which was exactly six years to the day after my initial biopsy surgery.

Dr. Forsythe told me that I would begin with six months

of heavy chemotherapy. I would go in for a 60cc cytoxin push, a huge slow injection of a very heavy-duty chemotherapy drug, followed by oral medications taken at home for a week, and then two weeks later I would go in for two intra-muscular shots of chemo. The first shot was in a saltwater solution; it was like getting stung by a wasp each time. This series of shots – the cytoxin and the intra-muscular – in the two-week period were termed "one dose." In the doctors eyes that made up one round of chemo. I learned that I had to ask for more specific details on what they were going to do each time I went in.

For the first four months, I didn't throw up after the cytoxin, but I would go to bed and experience terrible abdominal pain and achy joints as the minerals in my body and intestinal flora were being eaten away. I had to be very careful of what I ate. Some days all I could eat was saltines and cream of potato or mushroom soup. Raw food and cheese were too harsh for my system. I was filled with toxins, the ones I started with and ones that were being added. While on chemo, I realized that I had to eat whatever stayed down or allowed me to continue eating. I felt that the most important thing was that I should not lose my appetite, so I did what I had to. Popsicles became my best friends.

One night I had gotten up after a chemo treatment thinking that I might throw up; luckily I didn't, so I just went back to bed. When I started towards my bed, I saw an incredibly beautiful blue light filling the area where I had been lying, so I just crawled back into the wonderful, beautiful blue light. I thanked the angels that were always helping me as I fell into a peaceful sleep.

I tried to maintain focus and purpose knowing that this journey was part of my education, but there were always those difficult moments. The first time I took the two intra-muscular shots, Dr. Forsythe told me that to help curb the side effects, I needed to take some Tylenol and Benadryl. He didn't go into what the side effects were, and I didn't think to ask.

Jerry drove me home and I started cooking dinner. I had forgotten what Dr. Forsythe had said and thought if I did have any side effects, then I'd take the medicine. Wrong. I was standing over the sink cleaning some potatoes and I started to feel chilled, so I went and put on a robe. I took my Tylenol, and then before I knew what had hit me, I was shaking violently and absolutely freezing. Jerry called Dr. Forsythe and left word for him to call and then went to the store to pick up the Benadryl. While he was gone I sat on the couch under a pile of blankets shaking. The phone rang – it was my doctor. I was trying to tell him what was happening to me; I was scared. The shaking was so violent that I was hitting myself in the head with the phone and was afraid I was going to bite my tongue off as I spoke. He asked me if I had taken the Tylenol and Benadryl, and I told him no, but that it was on the way. He said he was pleased that the intra-muscular shots were working well and was sorry he hadn't told me what the side effects would be. Personally, I thought health care professionals did this intentionally, because if we really knew what would occur, we probably wouldn't take the treatments.

I had an electric mattress cover and I turned it on high and crawled under the covers. When Jerry got back from the store and brought the medicine in to me, I immediately took it. Then he crawled into bed beside me and held me tight trying to keep me warm and still. His holding me really helped me, even though I was still cold. Such devotion he had for me! He was sweating because the bed was so hot, but I felt like I was sitting on an iceberg. Jerry cooked for me, helped feed me, and did anything else that I needed. I rarely saw the sunlight on my days off, only the four walls of our bedroom. Then my weekend would end, and I would go back to work. I Thank God that those days seem so far away now, but even now occasionally a tear will slide down my cheek in memory of that excruciating pain and discomfort.

During these months, it was important for me to appear normal. I needed to think that everything was all right, so for four to five nights each week I'd get up and go to work and smile. All I could think about was just putting one foot in front of the other; anything more was overwhelming. The bosses, supervisors, and my fellow employees were great. I'd be standing at a table, and I'd have to ask to be pushed out (casino slang for relieved) because I couldn't stand another minute. I'd go get sick and sit down for five minutes, and then I'd be back at the table trying to pretend that everything was fine. It didn't matter how great the pain or how sick I was; I'd go to work and pretend that all was well. After my shift, I'd go home and collapse – that is if I didn't have to go the doctor's or the hospital.

Because of my concerns about hair loss, I spoke to other chemo patients, my doctor, and his nurses about when to start expecting my hair to fall out and how long it would be before I would be bald. Everyone said that it would take about two months and that some people didn't lose their hair at all. For me it took thirteen days! I was totally thrown off guard. One of the main reasons I didn't want to do chemo was because I didn't want to lose my beautiful, thick auburn hair. We're talking major trauma!

"Okay," I thought, "I'm going to plan my hair loss." Before I started chemo, I asked a girlfriend to come over and cut about six inches off my hair, which was halfway down my back. I thought that as my hair fell out, I'd just keep cutting it, shorter and shorter. In my mind, my hair was not just hair – it was the reason that people liked me and thought I was pretty. I was convinced I wasn't pretty, and therefore wasn't likable without my hair. My hair was beautiful, like a mane. Everyone always commented on Beth's beautiful, auburn hair. There was no way I could prepare for the devastation.

My bald head was like a war zone both inside and out. Until now my hair had been a huge part of my identity. Through losing my hair I had the opportunity to learn what Samson had learned many years earlier. My hair was not my strength, and my inner "I" had always been stronger than my hair, but only now would I learn this.

My hair first began falling out when I got up for work one day and went to take a shower. As I washed my hair, mounds of it fell into my hands. Excruciating pain filled me as I fell to my knees and began screaming and crying uncontrollably. This was more devastating than anything I had ever felt. Crying, I told Jerry my hair was falling out and that I had just flushed down toilet bowls full. He tried to calm me, telling me I must be exaggerating because I still had lots of hair, so I reached up and stroked my hand through my hair. He gasped as huge clumps of hair came off in my hand. I was afraid to brush or touch my hair, so I did a little shape-shifting by carefully placing the hairs in a feasible position so I could go to work that day. I remember standing at the game table with hair all over the front of my shirt and in the money tray. I was barely able to maintain my control emotionally. On my breaks I would go to the locker room and cry. I asked a friend of mine if she would go with me after work and help me pick out a wig. Now I can see how stupid it was of me to even go to work that day, but the need to appear to be okay was all-important.

I picked out a wig that matched my natural hair and style as closely as possible. I tried to make the outing fun, and I tried on lots of wigs. The woman who owned the shop was very helpful and made sure that both the quality and fit were good. There were still a lot of people at work who didn't know what was going on in my life and had no idea that I was wearing a wig; they thought I had gotten a perm! This was fine with me.

I felt so ashamed of losing my hair that I wouldn't even let Jerry see me without my wig. I remember how hot the wig was during the summer and how it always felt like I had a rug on my head, but despite my discomforts, I wouldn't take it off. I had a few scraggly hairs that were left on my head, and I found myself combing them over the top of my head as some balding men do. I used to think how silly such men looked, and would think, "Why won't they just trim the hair and not worry about a bald spot?" I swore from that day forward I would never make fun of another man combing his hair over to cover a bald spot.

Once a year, Eldorado, the casino I worked at, would give their employees a gift certificate to be used at one of their two expensive restaurants. Each year Jerry and I would plan a fun evening, starting with dinner at La Strada. This year was no exception. It was fun to really dress up; he was in a suit and I was in a red dress. After we parked the car, we headed towards the doors of the casino. The wind was blowing incredibly hard. All I could think about was that my wig might blow off, so while other women were worried about their dresses, I was worried about my hair! My dress had blown up over my head, but I didn't care. I was holding onto the wig! I know that it probably looked pretty funny with my dress flying everywhere, but all I was worried about was keeping my wig on.

I was getting used to my new daily routine. I would go in for the IV push and follow up with seven days of chemo pills and prednisone; then, after a week, I'd go in for the two intra-muscular shots. I'd wind up with about three good days out of the month where I felt somewhat normal. Being on all of those drugs all the time was hard. The first dose of chemo would start me vomiting. By that evening or early the next day, my body would ache all over and all I could eat was my saltines and soup. The prednisone that I took for one week turned me into "super bitch" and would keep me up all night. The intra-muscular shots threw me into major chills, fever, and violent shaking even though I always took my Tylenol and Benadryl.

Almost immediately when I began the chemo, I became aware of the numbness and loss of circulation in my hands and feet. My head would tingle, and a type of cradle cap was forming on my scalp. Fortunately, I knew about reflexology. Both in the hands and feet we have nerve endings that correlate with different areas and organs of the body. Reflexology works by applying certain massage techniques to these nerve endings, or pressure points, and the corresponding organ or body part is stimulated. I didn't have extra money for regular reflexology or massage treatments, so I bought a vibrator and massaged my feet and head every morning with the vibrator during the entire chemo ordeal. My hands were not strong enough to massage the pressure points, but while I was vibrating my feet and head, my hands were vibrated also. This process massaged the pressure points and increased the circulation. I recommend everyone going through chemotherapy should have a good vibrator. If you can go in for regular massages and reflexology, great. Daily stimulation to your extremities is necessary (and your head is included under extremities).

Even though Jerry was a great help to me, things always changed for the worse when his family came to visit. His father and two brothers came one winter. Jerry never could stand up to his family. One day his older brother was supposed to pick me up after work and take me home, but decided to change his plans without informing me. I got off work, exhausted as usual and just wanting to go home. After waiting thirty minutes and realizing that his brother was a "no show," I finally called Jerry to come and pick me up. Then as I was walking away from the phone, Jerry's brother walked up and casually asked me what time it was. I was so angry and tired that I blasted him good. I felt like ripping his head off. Prednisone will do that. He took off. When Jerry came, I told him what I had done, and he got furious at me. He said that his brother was very sensitive and had been up for days doing drugs and that I shouldn't be so hard on him. I thought I would explode right there. I blasted Jerry and told him that if he thought recreational drugs were tough, maybe he should try a shot of chemo and see how he felt then. This little bit of contention never completely mended, but fortunately this was the only major fight we ever had. I personally knew how difficult dealing with family could be, but I felt then and still do feel that Jerry should have stood up for me.

Dr. Forsythe had said that I would only need six months of chemo, but, as I was finding out, life is not what we always anticipate it to be. I wound up taking the strong chemo for seven months and then began a milder, or what I call medium, dose of chemo. It was a much smaller IV push, followed by the oral chemo and prednisone, but with no intra-muscular shots. This regimen allowed me more good and normal days between treatments, which was wonderful. I felt health would soon be returning. I was looking forward to being off chemo all together.

Within a few weeks after reducing my chemo, I began reaching out to different support groups, as well as attending different events sponsored by the local cancer organizations. One event was a fashion show for cancer patients. The object was to teach patients about the best way to wear wigs, scarves, and makeup. I had fun, met new people, and learned some good techniques for improving my appearance. Afterwards, I threw away my old tube of mascara and bought a hypoallergenic brand and took my wig into my hairdresser so she could trim it up so it would fit my face and look more like my natural hair.

Chapter 14

Opening New Doors

Never, never, never, never give up.
–Winston Churchill

I found it very difficult to admit that I needed psychological support, but clearly, I did. Starting to get out and meet with other cancer patients really helped me. At church, my grandparents heard about Bernie Siegel's book, titled *Love, Medicine & Miracles*, so they picked up a copy and mailed it to me. Shortly after reading it, I asked my doctor about any groups that specifically followed Bernie Siegel's program. He referred me to one person who then directed me to a woman named Sherri Rice, who ran a group at Washoe Medical Center. She and I continued our friendship into other groups and have remained very good friends. Her cancer support group closely followed Bernie Siegel's program.

When I first went, I was scared and shy. It was hard for me to speak up, and when I did I afraid that someone might think badly of me or judge me. Sherri always made me feel like a real person. She helped me realize that I was wonderful, and yes, a survivor. This wasn't a group where you played "poor, pitiful me." The group was a safe place to feel your pain and cry, but the point was to walk through your fears and come out feeling stronger and happier. In addition to Sherrie's group, I got to attend an all-day workshop in Reno with Bernie Siegel himself. Just listening to him was liberating for me. In my dreams, school was getting easier, but I was still in school.

Now that my self-esteem was improving, I was beginning to realize that I could not continue working in the casinos with all of that smoke. I'd talk myself out of leaving on those nights when the smoke wasn't so bad, but other nights, when there would be too much smoke, I knew I had to leave. The smoke was hurting my body, but I didn't know what to do. I had to continue to work in the casinos because of the health insurance, and besides, Jerry and I needed the money! I had always made more money than Jerry did, and, having bought a house together, we now had house payments to make. I didn't feel like I could quit my job, so I didn't.

Time had been passing, and I had been on chemo for eighteen months now. Dr. Forsythe said that I could be taken off chemo, not just medium chemo, but off chemo altogether. Hurrah! "With no more chemo, maybe I could make some changes in my work environment," I thought.

When I had been off chemo for six months, I began anticipating the day when I believed that my hair would be long enough to go without the wig. Finally, after much deliberation, I decided that the length of two inches would suffice. It felt great to not be wearing a wig, but I did feel like a little boy with this short, short hair. Still, I was uncertain if I could I go to work without a wig. Everyone was used to me with long hair, but a few of my friends encouraged me onward. I remember the first day I walked into work with my new hairdo. Coworkers from other shifts, who didn't know that I had been wearing a wig, could not believe that I had cut off all my hair. Others, who did know, told me I looked like a baby and was adorable. I appreciated their reassuring comments. This one elderly guy who worked on my shift had heard me tell someone that I thought I looked like a boy. He was so funny when he said, "You're the cutest little boy *I've* ever seen!"

I was glad to be off the chemo, but I would get nervous every time I had to go in for tests. I was always afraid that there might be something more. At six months without chemo, I began having some skin problems. After much consultation, the physicians decided the lymphoma was not staying in remission. Dr. Forsythe said that I needed a maintenance dose of chemo. He promised me that it was the mildest form of chemo and that all the doctors were hoping that the mild chemo would lock in my remission.
I went in for my supply of pills once every five weeks.

Prior to going on the mild chemo, I had decided to go back to school and get a degree so I could get out of the casinos. My girlfriend, Reva, was also thinking about going back to school because dealing cards was hard on her back. She already had one degree in costume design but was in the wrong city for that line of work. Reva knew that I wanted to go back to school, so she encouraged me to enroll in school with her. I agreed to take some classes. I didn't know what I wanted to study, but legal administration sounded stimulating. We would be going to school together, so we could study together. This would be fun!

I registered for the spring semester. Reva wound up never registering after all, but by then I was infected with the original enthusiasm. I liked school a lot and made good grades. School was another way of focusing on improving myself and keeping my mind from dwelling in the negativity of worry. I had it all planned out. I dropped to working the graveyard shift three days a week and attended school during the day. If I had exams, I would arrange with the doctor to postpone my chemo until after the tests. After slightly less than two years, I graduated with a 4.0 grade point average in the summer of 1991, six months sooner than I had planned. I was ecstatically proud of myself on graduation day. I had worked hard to obtain the education I needed to change professions.

Now that I had completed my education, it was time to quit the casino; I had to quit for my health. As my shift ended one morning, I decided that this was the right time to quit. I walked up to my boss and told him that I could not stand working in gaming any longer and that I was out of there. He told me not to be rash and told me that he would arrange for me to have a three-month medical leave so I could think about my decision. I took the medical leave and thanked him.

When my three months were up, I informed the casino that I would not be returning. I was trying to get my foot in the door of the legal community as a paralegal. I had sent out more than a hundred resumes and relentlessly followed them up with calls just trying to get in to introduce myself. It was hard. No one wanted to give me a break. You either had to know someone or be related to someone before an attorney would talk to you. I was able to hustle a few small contract jobs in the beginning. Then I decided to send a resume to an attorney who had a bad reputation for not being able to keep his employees because of his temper. Well, sure enough, he needed someone, and he begged me to come to work. The pay was terrible, but I learned a lot and it got my toe in the door. During this entire time, and for five months following graduation, I remained on mild chemo.

Even though I was on the mildest form of chemo, there were still side effects. Mostly, I experienced irritability and a sense of physical imbalance which affected my depth perception. I was also unable to sleep. During all these years of chemo, it had been difficult to sleep. *"Remember, Beth, you're on drugs, and drugs affect you this way."* I was tired of taking the drugs, and I was tired of being sick.

Chapter 15

Facing My Fear

Make believe you're brave; and the trick will take you far;
you may be as brave as you make believe you are....
— Rodgers and Hammerstein

After five months in the new job, early in May of 1992, when I was going in for my usual doctor's visit prior to starting my next dose of chemo, I decided to talk to Dr. Forsythe about when I could or would be taken off the drugs. I was tired and needed a rest. Altogether now I had been on chemo more than three years.

Jerry had begun balking about going with me to the doctors. He felt that since I wasn't in a critical stage, it wasn't necessary for him to go with me. He basically felt that everything was over, that it just was a question of another month or so, and I would be off all medication. I got really upset and told him that things weren't over because I was still going into the doctor's office or hospital every four to six weeks. I asked him to please continue to give me his support. Fortunately, he agreed when he understood my point.

Now I was ready to ask my doctor when all this madness would be over. Interestingly, my dreams about school were progressing. I was being told that my Ph.D. program was about to begin. Part of me was happy and yet I was concerned at the same time.

I went into the office and told Dr. Forsythe that I didn't want to take chemo anymore, that there must be another route, and that I was going to look into other options. I had always used everything I knew and looked for answers in any area to obtain health, and there were few limitations to what I would explore. Dr. Forsythe said that if I never wanted to take chemo again or see him again that I might want to consider a bone-marrow transplant. I was completely taken aback; this was my worst nightmare. Dr. Forsythe and I had become very close and he was very supportive of me and my beliefs, and because of this I trusted his opinion. He explained that the lymphoma was being very stubborn and wasn't staying in remission and that I could take my time to think about the bone-marrow transplant and review my options.

Having quit my original paralegal position earlier, I had been on a legal temp job that morning and felt obligated to return to work after my doctor's visit. I could hardly concentrate on work but at the same time was trying to act like nothing was wrong. At the end of the day, the attorneys asked if I would come in on Saturday. I made an excuse of previous plans and clocked out for the day. As I rode the elevator down, I was fighting back tears. I had an appointment with a friend, Tanzy, to have some bodywork done. As I got in my car and headed for my appointment, I started crying and I couldn't stop, and at times I could hardly see the road. When I arrived, Tanzy asked me what was wrong. All I could do was wail through the whole session, but I got enough words out that she knew what was going on. It was during this session that I forgave my mother for what she had done.

This was my sixth of a series of thirteen Hellerwork bodywork sessions with Tanzy. I had chosen Hellerwork because it was an offshoot of, and very similar to, Rolfing. The belief held by many bodyworkers is that the body holds the memories of past traumas in the fascial tissue (a type of connective tissue) of the body and the tissue becomes rigid.

During and right after my Hellerwork session I realized that I should follow through with the bone-marrow transplant. Once I had made this discussion, I also knew that it didn't matter what had occurred in the past with my mother. Now I knew I needed her, and somehow I wanted to bridge the gap and start fresh. I knew that a single act is not the sum total of who a person is.

So, I felt I was able to forgive my mother, but needed to find a way for us to talk. My older sister, Debbie, was organizing a baby shower for our younger sister, Robyn. I knew that I wouldn't be able to attend but I had sent a gift to my sister's house for her to take to the party. In addition, I had asked Debbie if she would call me from the baby shower after the gifts were opened so that I could talk to Robyn and everyone. I said that if Momma wanted to talk to me, I would be open to talking with her. Debbie called me during the baby shower and announced that I wanted to talk to everyone. I could hear my mother asking, "Debbie, are you sure she wants to talk to everyone?"

"Yes, and you're getting on the phone and talking to her," Debbie replied.

We both started crying right after I said "Momma," and she said, "Bethie." Yes, we were both nervous, but we were both willing to forgive and let go. With my heart pounding, I told her that I needed her and that I was going in for a bone-marrow transplant.

Within a matter of days, Momma had arranged for me to fly back to Dallas for a week's visit before starting my next round of "spiritual growth." Even though my birthday wasn't until December and it was the summertime, my family had a birthday/welcome home party for me. It felt so good to be close to family again. I realized that I wanted the option of seeing my family more frequently. I thought about moving so that I would be living closer to them, though perhaps not in the same city. I had lost a lot of weight and was looking pretty bad, but my mother and siblings loved me anyway. Now I was ready to go back to Reno and complete my next task. Even though I was acting as if I were going to go through with the bone-marrow transplant, in my heart I wanted to give myself a few days to process my thoughts and feelings.

Chapter 16

No Simple Answer

In a dark time, the eye begins to see
—Theodore Roethke

I had been through nine years of painful struggle for the sake of growth, knowledge, and healing. I had looked into many avenues, both alternative and traditional means of healing my body, mind and spirit. I had learned more about myself and life than I probably would have learned in sixty years, had I not gotten ill, but there was always more to learn. My mind was reeling; I didn't know if I could handle anything more.

In 1983 I had believed that undergoing a bone-marrow transplant would kill me, and now I was faced with that same choice. I saw that I had two choices. Behind door number 1, I had a horrific nightmare, and behind door number 2, I had a horrific nightmare. I could decide against the transplant and remain on chemo for an indefinite period of time, hoping that I would not get worse and die five years down the line. Or, I could undergo the transplant, still with no guarantee on whether I would die or not. Either way, I didn't want to die; I wasn't ready to leave, but there was no simple answer.

I made the decision in less than a week that I should at least go down to Palo Alto, California, a five-hour drive from Reno, and talk to the doctors at Stanford University about the possibility of a transplant. I called Dr. Forsythe and told him that I would go to Stanford. I wasn't making a decision yet; I was just leaving all options open.

Dr. Forsythe said he would contact the doctors he knew there and see if he could pull any weight to accelerate the process. Next, I had to get approval from Jerry's insurance company. (Which was now the source of my health insurance.) Dr. Forsythe fixed that by referring me to Stanford University for a second opinion. I had been so far down this road now that somehow I knew it was time to go ahead with the transplant. I wanted to be done with doctors and hospitals. I thought I'd try this one last drastic measure and then hopefully no more doctors.

I felt I would be approved by Stanford as a good candidate for a transplant, but I had some concern about my weight. Over the last year I had lost a lot of weight because the lymphoma aggravated my stomach and intestines. I was hardly able to hold down any food, and was always vomiting. I was much too weak. I would sit and cry all the time and I didn't even know why. I knew, one way or another, I would have to put some weight back on before going through the transplant.

My dad was working for Ross Laboratories, so I asked him if he could get me some Ensure Plus, a high-protein supplemental drink. He sent seven cases. I began drinking two cans a day plus eating many small meals, trying to stretch my stomach so I could increase my food intake. I had to practically force-feed myself, but it was working. I needed to gain at least twenty pounds, I'm 5'6" and my weight was down to 104 pounds. A month after my last visit with Dr. Forsythe, both Stanford and the insurance company approved my visit, and a date was arranged for my initial consultation on June 29, 1992.

I reconnected with Sherri Rice, my therapist, and asked if she would privately counsel me because I needed so much help in remaining mentally strong. I knew now more than ever I had to strengthen both mind and spirit and chose to reduce my working hours to part-time. I thought I had already strengthened my mind pretty well, but I had no idea what truly lay ahead.

On my first visit with Sherri I asked if she could connect me to an organization so I could do a little volunteer work. Because I enjoyed children, I asked to work with them until I went into the hospital. She was on the board of CAPP (Child Assault Prevention Program) whom she referred me to after notifying CAPP that I would be calling. The people in the office were outstanding, and I found myself helping them with not only the educational program that we took to the schools but also with general office work. The programs that we took to the schools were skits to teach kids to protect themselves.

One day I was working with a new facilitator named Sharon, and in part of the skit she reached up to stroke my hair. She didn't know I had a wig on. When she went to reach for my hair, I whispered, "Don't touch my hair; it might fall off." She never batted an eye and casually patted my leg in place of touching my hair. Afterwards I filled her in on the details. It was then that I learned how startled she had been to find out that I was wearing a wig. That made me feel better about my appearance.

For me, working with the kids kept my own spark glowing while keeping my mind occupied so I wouldn't dwell on fears and worries. Some kind of healthy diversion is always good for the soul.

Chapter 17

A Knight Worth Remembering

No one ever finds life worth living,
he has to make it worth living.
—Author Unknown

The day arrived for Jerry and me to make the first trip to Stanford University Hospital, and we determined that this wasn't going to be a trip of just testing and hospitals. We were going to have some fun. Jerry made plans for romance on the beach, saying that we would be stopping at Stanford for a side trip and then, "Off to the beach!" We drove to Stanford University Hospital, found the correct department, and began the initial second opinion and consultation.

Before I could even be seen by a doctor I was sent down to x-ray, then to have lots of blood drawn, and finally, of course, to fill out and sign endless forms. Then, after all this, the receptionist handed me a folder with information on everything I might have ever wanted and needed to know about the transplant procedure. She asked me to read the entire folder of information before I returned for the consultation in the afternoon, by which time the doctors would have reviewed my blood test results.

There was a very pretty outdoor mall less than a mile from the hospital, so Jerry and I decided to eat there and then spend some time walking around the mall and enjoying its beautiful flowers. This was a nice break from the sterile walls and the aroma of rubbing alcohol that awaited us back at the hospital.

When we returned, we were placed in a cubicle to wait. Various people came by to introduce themselves and explain their part in the procedure. First, there was a scheduling person, then a clinical social worker, and then the many doctors of different nationalities that were all in training. Everyone was extremely nice and completely willing to explain anything and everything. These people went the extra mile. Their attitudes and personalities were completely opposite those of the doctors I had encountered in the beginning. I was a real person, treated compassionately. It was amazing – from the receptionist to the doctors, everyone gave hundred percent to help me. All the staff members expressed devotion and joy towards their work. What a difference from my experience at Parkland!

I finally saw a doctor, Dr. Long, and he came with his entourage of visiting physicians. Each physician introduced himself to me, participated in the explanation of the procedure, and answered my questions. I brought a tape recorder, at the suggestion of the staff, for the dual purpose of going back over the information and to help me formulate any additional questions that might come up later. I really got it that the bone-marrow transplant department and its staff look at many different factors to determine who falls into the "good candidate" profile for the procedure. I qualified as a "good candidate" in large part because I had inner strength and a lot of outside support.

When I asked what percentage my chance of success would be, the doctors told me I had a sixty percent success ratio. I needed to figure this ratio stuff out, so I asked them to tell me what was the highest percentage success ratio that they ever gave a person. They all said seventy percent was the highest success rate, except in very rare instances in which they gave an eighty to ninety percent success rate.

They stated that this higher ratio had only been given once or maybe twice. My mind and I began our own conversation and we decided that their seventy percent really meant hundred percent, so the sixty percent that I was quoted was actually ninety percent. It made perfect sense to me, and I added a few more points because I knew of my determination to have health! The doctors tried briefly to talk me out of my reasoning, but I just smiled and said, "You don't know who you're dealing with."

Jerry and I left the hospital late that afternoon and headed south of Santa Cruz to Seaside, a resort town about halfway between Santa Cruz and Monterey. We rented a honeymoon suite, which included a jacuzzi tub, in a quiet little hotel about a block from the beach. After checking in, we went to the hotel's seafood restaurant. It was about twenty minutes before closing. We were completely surprised by how nice both the atmosphere and service were. The food was absolutely delicious. After filling our stomachs as well as our senses with pleasurable memories, we went back to our room and filled the tub with lots of bubbles and soaked our bodies and souls with the pleasure of the moment. We drifted off to sleep in a sweet, intimate embrace.

The next morning, Jerry continued his endeavors to keep my mind off cancer, doctors and hospitals. He woke me up at dawn and, in my sleepy state, whisked me off to the beach; he said that we needed to look for sand dollars before the pelicans could get to them. For a moment or two I was just sleepwalking, but the sand between my toes and the morning breeze off the ocean woke me lovingly.

I slowly strolled along the water's edge as the sun fully rose and then stopped to give homage to the gods. At first, it looked as though we were too late. The sand dollars we were finding had already been broken, but I kept looking knowing that I would find one intact. Sure enough I found one, and then I found another one. As I was walking back to show Jerry my treasures, I stopped and hollered that I thought I had found another one. This one was a lovely rose-purple color. I had not seen one like this before. Jerry came over and picked it up; it was alive. I was thrilled. I told him to throw it back, and set it free, which he did. The sand dollars were a sign to me from the heavens that everything would be okay. I knew that I would live. I brought the two sand dollars home with me and placed them in a special place as my daily reminder of my special message.

Chapter 18

Focus, Focus, Focus

*Your work is to discover your work, and then with all
your heart to give yourself to it.*
—Buddha

I received my second opinion from Stanford. Now Dr.
Forsythe had to present my case to the insurance company
for approval of the bone-marrow transplant. While this
approval process was going on, I was to go back to Reno
and have two months of regular (strong) chemo in preparation
for the harvest and transplant of the bone marrow.

I now had insurance only through Jerry's employer.
Bally's, the casino that Jerry was working for, had begun
bankruptcy proceedings, so my approval for the consultation
and chemo was now denied, and the benefits were never
paid for the second opinion and the chemo. Bally's was sold
to Hilton. This merger also meant Jerry's health insurance
changed. We needed an HMO to pay for my medical
expenses. Casinos were changing insurance carriers yearly,
but because of this, you couldn't be denied due to any
preexisting conditions. At least we were sure hoping that
this was still the case. Bally's had carried an HMO, but a
few months before they were sold, they had dropped the
HMO and bought a poorer quality insurance, which failed
to pay my initial bill to Stanford and Dr. Forsythe. When
Hilton had full ownership, they brought back an HMO. It
was good that we had access to an HMO again, but now we

had to seek approval for the transplant with the new insurance company. Life was thrilling enough without walking on the edge working with the insurance companies also. I had already completed my two months of chemo, in addition to a six-weeks' break without chemo when my approval finally arrived. We had to move quickly. I was at that ripened place that the doctors were wanting me to be in order to begin the more serious techniques in preparation for the transplant.

The date was set for me to begin the long process of a BONE-MARROW TRANSPLANT. My grandparents and Jerry's brother together sent enough money to pay all of our bills for the next three months. The employees of the graveyard shift at the Eldorado threw a party for me and came bearing gifts of nightgowns, robes, books, posters and a lap blanket. I typed up my itinerary for the next few months and mailed it out so everyone would have the necessary information about procedure, dates, phone numbers, and addresses. I set up a schedule for my immediate family members to be with me at the hospital. My grandparents were scheduled for the first and longest shift, the first two weeks; and then my dad and step-mother, my nana (my other grandmother), my brother, my mother, my sister Debbie, and my sister Becky were all scheduled for varying lengths of time. Between Jerry and my family, I had almost continuous support. Jerry would be there for three or four days each week and then would drive back to Reno and work on the other days. Even though I arranged all the details around my hospital stay, I still don't know who watched the animals while Jerry was gone – probably a neighbor.

I even called my sister Debbie and asked her if she could get one of my favorite comedian's (Sinbad) address. I knew that celebrities sometimes would respond to sick people's requests. We never got his address, but I didn't worry about it. Jerry had taped a couple of Sinbad's comedy skits, along with those of a few other comedians like Bill Cosby and Rita Rudner. I knew the importance of laughter both in healing and keeping my spirits lifted during the tough times.

After the approval from the second insurance company, it was time to continue with the preliminary steps. Part of the preliminary work was the last two months of chemo, but now I had to have another bone-marrow aspiration (like the one I had in 1983), and two other tests – a lymphangeogram and a CT scan. The bone-marrow aspiration and CT scan were to be done in Reno at Washoe Medical Center and the lymphangeogram was to be done at Stanford.

On the advice of a fellow transplantee, I insisted on drugs from my doctor before undergoing the aspiration. The unbelievable pain of my first aspiration years before was still chiseled in my mind, and I felt nervous and terrified. My doctor prescribed two pills that were supposed to be "super-duper" pain pills. I was to take one or both one hour before the procedure. I took the first pill about an hour and a half before my dreaded aspiration, but after forty minutes, I felt nothing, so I took the second one.

After we finished lunch at an ice cream and sandwich parlor, Jerry drove me to the hospital. From his bone-marrow aspiration kit, the doctor laid out his instruments in the little stainless steel tray. I was asked to change into one of those drafty hospital gowns, which I refused to do. I had worn a large t-shirt and leggings and explained that I would just roll down the waistband. The doctor was concerned about getting blood on my clothes. I thanked him for his concern and told him that I would not change. As soon as I lay face down on the table, I began to cry and shake. All I could remember was the pain and horror of this same procedure nine years earlier. The doctor was concerned with my uncontrollable tears and blurted out to Jerry, "I haven't even touched her yet." Jerry held my hand and talked to me while I cried throughout the entire procedure. This aspiration went much faster than the one nine years earlier. Even so, I was waiting for that rush of "Thank goodness, it's over." My hip hurt, but I would live.

My adrenaline was flowing full tilt. I asked Jerry if he would take me to the rock shop so I could walk around for a little bit. Rocks always made me feel better, so off to the Comstock Rock Shop we went. After I had walked around for maybe ten minutes my adrenaline began to dissipate and the pain pills were then able to medicate. I advised Jerry that I should get home fast. When I got home I was almost comatose; exhaustion from the emotional trauma had drained me I wasn't even able to raise my head off the pillow for twenty-four hours. It's amazing what adrenaline can accomplish!

The next day, I woke up in absolute jubilation. I told a dear friend that everyone should have to go in and have a bone-marrow aspiration because, if they did, they would realize how precious life was, and they would be happier.

The following night I had a dream where I was surrounded by my angels and guides. They informed me that my dissertation was to begin. I awoke feeling overwhelmed *"Oh, goody, does this mean more fun?!"* I thought sarcastically. I was hoping that these "school" dreams would be coming to some kind of closure by now.

Chapter 19

Angels in Disguise

*We all have the extraordinary coded within us. . .
waiting to be released.*
—Jean Houston

Along my healing journey, so many people were coming
forward with help and support, each one an angel and a
blessing. It was also becoming clear that I would be in the
hospital on Thanksgiving, my birthday, Christmas and New
Year's, but I might possibly be home by my wedding
anniversary in February. Realizing what I would miss, my
friend, Cathy, decided she would prepare a celebration feast
and bring it to my house before I went into the hospital. This
proved to be a celebration above all others! Cathy prepared
the most delicious and the largest spread of holiday foods
that I've ever seen. There was turkey and dressing, potatoes,
sweet potatoes, a vegetable and pasta casserole, homemade
cranberry sauce, rolls, pie, and lots of love. It was the most
wonderful meal that I had ever eaten, and I was amazed that
she had done all of this for me.

Cathy was a hygienist at my dentist's office. She had
been with Dr. Stewart's office for just about six months
when I went in for a cleaning and pre-exam, prior to my
hospitalization. The pre-exam was to determine everything
that needed to be done. For instance, all of my cavities had
to be filled. My mouth had to be in tiptop shape before the
bone-marrow transplant. During my cleaning, I became

"doctored out." Cathy was cleaning my teeth, and I just couldn't handle anything else that day. I was mentally and emotionally exhausted and broke down crying, explaining that I had to leave. My dentist, who knew my history, came in and told me not to worry because he completely understood. He told me that his daughter had, at a very early age, also undergone chemo for a number of years. The next day Cathy called to make sure that I was all right and to find out if she had done something wrong. I explained that I was about to go into the hospital and was just on overload. After so many years of illness and doctors, I had battle fatigue. We've been friends ever since.

By now, I had put on about fifteen pounds. I was feeling stronger, and I felt more comfortable with going through the next procedure. I had never had a lymphangeogram before but was promised that it wasn't as traumatic as the bone-marrow aspiration. I learned that there are two ways of performing a lymphangeogram. One is by an incision in the top of the foot and the other is through an incision between the toes.

You may not think I'm lucky, but it always amazes me how lucky I am. The day that Jerry and I drove to Stanford for the lymphangeogram was just a few days after the bone-marrow aspiration. The person who was scheduled to perform the lymphangeogram had called in sick. A woman who was considered the best in administering this procedure was called into work as the replacement. She was good, and the only part that hurt was the initial Novocaine shot. I had to lie very still while a very tiny needle was placed in the lymphatic vein and dye was slowly injected. After both feet were done, I had to wait for the dye to travel up my lymphatic vessels before the x-rays were taken. The dye outlined the path of the lymphatic system, and the x-ray showed if there were any obstructions or swelling. Then, in the next couple of weeks, I would be going in for the bone-marrow harvest and catheter placement.

During these last few months of preliminary workup I was going in weekly for private therapy sessions with Sherrie Rice to help me deal with what was occurring in my life. I would discuss my dreams, visions, and fears. This work was extremely helpful in keeping me focused on what I was going through and in maintaining and improving the strength of my spirit. I never quit reaching out and searching in any direction, whether alternative or traditional.

Avenues and doors continued to open up for me. My friend Laurice had shared some information with me on toning. I had always believed in the power of sound, but I found out that I was not using it to its full extent. Through her help, I began vocalizing my pain and grief. I was clearing as much as possible. I had to get to the core of the thought processes which had created the image of disease.

Early in my diagnosis I had heard of psychic surgery but had never had the opportunity to experience it. Now, years later, the opportunity arose, and I decided to try a session. Just like with anything else new, the uncertainty was scary for me. Two weeks before I went into the hospital for the bone-marrow harvest and catheter implant, I drove out to a woman's house for one of the most incredible healing experiences I had ever encountered.

Connie and her husband had turned their barn into a church that was brightly painted with angels and clouds. In the back was her healing room. After attending the church service and singing along with Elvis (on tape) and the woman's dog, I and fifty or so other people each took a turn in the healing room. I had never experienced anything like that before. This person was a real-life, honest-to-goodness, legitimate psychic surgeon. She had me lay on the table while she gently moved her hands over my body. I witnessed actual physical matter being removed from my body. I watched and felt, without pain, as my fears and disease were being removed. I left the church humbled and grateful for all the wonders that crossed my path.

As I drove home I was in absolute bliss watching light emanate from the mountains, trees, people, and animals, as well as from many inanimate objects. I saw God in everything. I was beginning to feel as if I had done something right. All of these people wanted to reach out and help me! I felt myself move through a gate that opened in only one direction, and that direction felt more sane and grounded than I had been in previous events in my life. Daily I was amazing myself with my inner strength. There was a continuous flow of positive support, and I was always able to rise above whatever obstacle was thrown my way.

In my dreams my angels and guides walked with me hand in hand and told me that I still needed to proceed with the bone-marrow transplant. They often did not give reasons, this I knew from past experience with them, so I surrendered to trust.

With my new awakening, it was important to me to be rebaptized. I made arrangements with a local Christian Science church that I had attended a few times. The church reminded me of a Unity church I had attended with my mother back in high school. The ceremony was with just Jerry, me, and the minister. The minister performed a beautiful baptism. There was no "dunking." She dipped a white rose into the holy water and then blessed me by touching the wet white rose to my forehead, throat, and heart. By the end of ceremony, Jerry, the minister, and I were all crying. Jerry and I felt we needed to continue in the sacred moment, so, afterwards, we drove over the mountains to Tahoe for lunch and then back home for a quiet evening.

Chapter 20

The Time Is Now

*In nature things move violently to their place
and calmly to their place.*
—Francis Bacon

I was going through my checklist of everything I needed
to do in preparation for my admission to Stanford Hospital.
I called my mother asking for suggestions or feedback. My
mother suggested that it would be a good idea to write a
good-bye letter to the cancer – that through writing the letter
I could fully let go, and through letting go, I would achieve
the healing and health that I so desired. This was an
interesting concept, to write a letter to one's dis-ease, and I
decided to try it.

As I began writing. I was surprised to realize that the
cancer had been a friend and not an enemy. The cancer and
the experience it carried had taught me many things over the
years. I thanked the cancer experience for everything that I
learned and told it that it must go now, because it was no
longer required for my learning process. I realized that I had
internalized my fears, insecurities and lack of self-
confidence, which, in turn, wreaked havoc on my physical
body, as well as on my mental, emotional and spiritual bodies.

I knew that I was ready to heal because following my
letter of good-bye and gratitude, I had a dream that
indicated to me that I was ready for the transplant.

I was on a ship at sea, and another ship had taken our ship hostage. There were people patrolling to make sure that no one escaped. I could see the shore a long way off, and someone had said that there was no other escape besides swimming to shore. I said that I would do it and bring help. In all my years of dreaming, I would never jump into water; it did not matter how inviting the water looked. I could see whales and other sea creatures swimming. I was scared but decided I could swim without making a disturbance in the water and could make it to the shore safely. I jumped in and began swimming.

The next morning I woke up and knew that I was ready. My last appointment with Sherri was the day before I was to be admitted for the harvesting. I shared my dream with her and told her that I was now ready. Jerry and I drove down to Stanford for the bone-marrow harvest. The harvest was to be November 10, 1992, but when we arrived at the hospital, the surgical administration department discovered they had made a clerical error. I had been scheduled to be the first one into the operating room, but another person had been taken first. The surgeon advised me not to have the surgery because the process that the marrow had to undergo after aspiration and prior to storage was critical and required several hours. I didn't want any technicians falling asleep and messing up my marrow, so Jerry and I drove the five hours back home. We were to return to Stanford on Friday, November 13, 1992. Friday the 13th. Was this lucky or what?

When Jerry and I arrived again at Stanford, I found out that I would be kept overnight. I wasn't really happy, but I settled in for the stay. After I filled out more paperwork, the anesthesiologist began trying to find a vein that wouldn't collapse.

After many attempts, they were finally able to put me to sleep. I woke up in my hospital room in such pain. If I even tried to move an inch, I hurt. My poor arm was filled with holes from all the attempts to find a vein, and my backside was even worse with the bruising and hundreds of little holes that had been made to aspirate a pint of marrow. I didn't need a donor because they could use my own marrow in the type of transplant I was receiving.

After I received assistance using the portable toilet that was brought to my bedside, Jerry gave me a bouquet of flowers. Saturday afternoon I was released from the hospital and allowed to go home, so I passed my flowers over to the woman in the next bed. I thought I could go home, but there were always detours. Before our departure Saturday, I was wheeled into the apheresis unit to begin my first dose of 480 mg GCSF. The GCSF was to stimulate my body to mass-produce stem cells. Jerry was to inject me with this medicine every day over the next two days until we returned Monday morning. So we drove home to Reno Saturday night. On Monday I would begin apheresis, which could extend from three to five days, depending on whether or not enough stem cells had been collected.

The drive home was horrible. I couldn't get comfortable because of all the holes and bruising on my gluteus maximus, not to mention the discomfort of the Hickman catheter hanging out of my chest. I was afraid to even move my left arm because of the catheter. Inside and out, my whole body hurt. To top it off, Jerry would have to pull off the road about every thirty minutes because I kept throwing up.

Monday came way too soon, and we were back on the road again headed for Stanford to begin apheresis. By now I had had two GCSF shots. Upon arrival at the apheresis unit, I was hooked up to a machine by my catheter and watched as my blood was drawn out and passed through the tubes separating my stem cells from the rest of my blood. Of course, the remainder of my blood went back into my body. The stem cells were much lighter in color than the blood, more pinkish white. I got cold during apheresis, and had tingling sensations. The nurse explained that this was because when the blood was returned to my body, it was cooler than when it was removed. The nurse also had a huge bottle of Tums that she said I should chew when I got chilled or started to get muscle cramps. These were some of the side effects. Luckily, after the second session of apheresis on Tuesday, they had enough stem cells. The doctors explained that my stem cells were gathered as a back-up in case the bone marrow didn't take.

The following morning I had an appointment with the radiation department, and after that, Jerry and I would be granted passage back to Reno. We arrived at the hospital bright and early in hopes of completing the appointment quickly and getting home. I was already sick and tired of the doctors, but I also knew that the real fun (ordeal) was only about to begin.

More departments, more procedures. Yes, the technicians were nice, but enough was enough. At my first stop in radiology, they explained the radiation procedure. Then, measurements had to be taken for lead lung plates which would be used during the total body radiation. It was during this lung-plate measurement that the nurses explained that they would be giving me a pin-size dot tattoo in both the front and back of my body. The tattoo would be in the little hollow above my sternum, and this mark would serve as the point of reference to center the radiation machine. "No way, you are not giving me a tattoo!" I was not going to spend the rest of my life looking at this black dot every morning knowing that it would soon turn green. Everyone, including Jerry, was trying to persuade me to cooperate with being tattooed. Two nurses and my husband were all going to get tattoos first to show me that it would be okay. I told them that they could get all the tattoos they wanted, but I was not going to do it. My arms were crossed and I glared defiantly at them. Plain and simple, "NO." At this point, we were all upset, but I was not going to do it.

The supervisor of the department walked in about this time and asked what the problem was. The nurses explained to her that I wouldn't cooperate with procedure. She didn't even bat an eye; she said that they would just handle it the same way that they do for children and handed me a Sharpie pen. I just had to re-mark the dot every day until the radiation treatments were completed. I was happy. Daily I re-marked both the dot and the lines which were the guidelines for the lung plates. For the next week and a half I could draw lines on myself. Cool . . . at least it washed off!

Once the dilemma of the tattoo was resolved, I went down to radiology to meet the radiologists who would actually be running the x-ray machine. The radiologists further explained to me the process of administering radiation. Even though the process had been explained to me, it didn't really hit home until I actually went in and experienced the treatments. I was to stand on a platform with a harness attached to me that was hooked into the ceiling so if I passed out, I wouldn't fall. Then a metal wall would be dropped down behind me, with handles at my side to hold on to for support, and, finally, a Plexiglas door would be pulled shut within inches of my nose. And all the while these cold, lead lung-plates would be on my bare chest. The apparatus looked like a vertical coffin, and I was terrified.

After listening to the radiologists and briefly standing in my coffin to get the feel of it, I was asked to wait a minute while the technicians checked on the dates that I was to begin. Of course, I didn't wait; instead, I followed behind them into their office. Completely unaware of my presence, they discussed my case while I listened. One of the technicians said that my radiation would begin on Sunday, November 22nd. I wasn't even supposed to check in until Monday afternoon the 23rd. I went ballistic! How dare these people not even consult me? I was screaming and crying and shouted that I would not be treated like some lab rat. Each day that I could be at home before I was actually checked in for the long haul was so very precious to me, and nothing or no one was going to take this from me! Many people tried to quietly and quickly escort me into a room away from other patients and passersby. I was spilling my heart and soul out in agony. The radiologists explained that they had rescheduled me to accommodate their schedule since their department would be closed on Thanksgiving Day, and because of this I would just have to check in a day earlier so I would be finished with my radiation by Thanksgiving. I told them in no uncertain terms that this was a 24-hour establishment and that they would have to just make sure that someone was here because I would not come in early. Barbara, the clinical transplant coordinator, was in tears trying to work things out, and I was angry, hurt and out of control. It is amazing what can be worked out when a resolution must be reached. Sure enough, I didn't have to come in a day early and radiology didn't have to work on Thanksgiving. What we worked out was that I would check in about two hours early, which I agreed to. As we were driving out of town, I began feeling guilty for jumping on Barbara and had Jerry stop so I could call the hospital and apologize to her.

Chapter 21

Entering the Vision

*The future enters into us, in order to transform
itself in us, long before it happens.*
—Rainer Maria Rilke

Twenty years earlier, when I was thirteen, I had had a vision of lying in a hospital bed on the brink of life and death. My family members had gathered around in support and to say, "I love you." Now, on November 23, 1992, I checked into Stanford University Hospital for the long haul. The months of prep work had finally been completed, and it was time to proceed. My friends and family had rallied by my side. Nine years had passed since this whole cancer experience had first begun, and now I was facing the toughest part of all. I had signed papers attesting to my sixty percent chance of survival and to the fact that I would most definitely be sterile and would probably undergo menopause. I had always wanted to have a baby, and this was probably the most difficult thought of all to accept. I shed buckets of tears for a never-to-be-conceived child.

As I admitted myself into the hospital, I looked back over the last nine years; it felt like I had been in training for the Olympics and that today was the first day of the games. As the tension in the air increased, I could almost even hear the announcer say, "Let the games begin."

My grandparents had flown in for this traumatic event the day before. The four of us went to the hospital together, and I took care of my pre-check in. Afterwards, we went to enjoy my last supper before admittance. I chose the Olive Garden and consumed anything and everything I wanted, knowing that hospital food would be my menu for quite some time. I munched on flavorful hot garlic bread and lingini, savoring each bite. I then returned to the hospital to immediately check into my room in CHU (Compromised Host Unit – the host, my body, was compromised) to begin a hydration process before my first total body radiation treatment. While being hydrated through my IV catheter I began decorating my room so it would have a homey feel. I had posters of horses, kittens, waterfalls, flowers, and one to color with a big box of markers. Beside my bed I had rocks and feathers, and on the window sill I had candles. Jerry hooked up our VCR and then placed a box of videos underneath. Finally, I placed a beautiful red blanket at the foot of the bed. The nurses came in and hung a large thirty-day calendar starting with November 23, 1992, on the wall under the TV to mark the calendar with statistics as well as stars and other stickers representing the holidays.

During the hour of my first hydration, we actually got a lot done before I was taken down to the dungeon for my first treatment. The attendant who came to get me was very friendly and took extra care and talked to me. His special treatment was the same for all the patients, and it was so comforting. He would take me the quickest way down to radiology and return along a quieter route. He always had a smile on his face and a joke on his lips.

On this first trip, as with many of my trips, Jerry or Pap came down to radiology with me. When I arrived for my first total-body radiation treatment I was placed in my vertical coffin with the cold lung plates in place. All the while, tears were rolling down my face. I was terrified. The attendants explained that they could watch me through a camera, and if I needed to stop, all I had to do was tell them. While grateful for the option, I had no intention of delaying the process any longer than necessary. I had thought long and hard about the best approach in handling this situation. I chose to use an angel visualization and to ask for the angels' help. One angel was behind me holding me up, and another one stood in front of me while Christ outstretched his hands and protected my ovaries. A fourth angel wrapped its wing around the radiation machine with the radiation coming out of its wing in the form of white light entering my body. The whole time I repeated the Lord's prayer over and over. I just cried and prayed.

As always with doctors, their version of "one" and mine were different. I was to have four treatments a day with an additional one to my rib cage. With every session, there were three zaps, each causing me to tremble. Remember, it's always good to ask what the number one really means to your doctor; it actually could be *two, three,* or *four.*

Each night after everyone would leave, I would journal the day's events, or try to. I had actually begun journaling this adventure a few months before, but now when I was on medication sometimes the writings didn't make sense. After a while, I wasn't able to journal. Not only did my eyes or hands not work, but my sentences were making less and less sense. I would be writing about the day and then would go into being afraid that I would be kidnapped by my father.

For the most part, I went through the radiation pretty well and with minimal side effects. I threw up only once, after a few days of the total-body treatments. And on my third day, when I went in for my second treatment, I almost passed out. I felt so weak and I thought I might faint. Although my body was shaking, I told myself not to worry, that my angels were holding me. The nurses and doctors were surprised that I didn't lose my appetite and that I wasn't throwing up more. The vomiting definitely came later but not with the radiation. Only the diarrhea.

One day when Pap and I returned from radiology, Pap noticed that a happy birthday sticker had been placed on my calendar on December 2nd. He called the nurse in and explained that my birthday was December 7th, not the 2nd, but the nurse informed him that the 2nd would be my special birthday. That would be the day that my bone marrow would be transplanted, or returned back to me.

To my delight Dr. Forsythe sent me a floral arrangement that arrived shortly after I checked in. Stanford's preliminary paperwork had informed me that I would not be able to have any plants due to the possibility of germs in the room, and I had informed everyone I knew, but I hadn't thought to tell Dr. Forsythe. My flowers had to be kept at the nurses' station, so when I walked the halls, I could enjoy them. They were gorgeous, with many colors including three light pink/peach tulips. Everyone enjoyed my flowers. As Jerry left the hospital for his return trip to Reno, he took one of the tulips out of the bouquet and placed it beside him for his drive home.

Before entering the hospital, I had called Mike, a voluntary support person who had been referred to me because he had undergone the same bone-marrow procedure a year or two before. He was very kind and offered any and all information upon my request. He was the one who had advised me to ask for drugs prior to my second bone-marrow aspiration. I was so surprised when I came back from radiology and the nurses said Mike was in my room waiting to say "hi." He came to the hospital twice a year bringing his homemade lasagna for the nurses and visiting with a patient or two. He had intentionally planned this visit during my hospital stay. In addition, a few of my friends were also able to visit for a day or two. They later called me asking how I was doing after their visit, and I had to admit that I didn't remember that they had been there. No one's feelings got hurt, thank goodness. I was amazed by the amount of support both from people I knew as well as from people I didn't know. If there is anyone who doesn't know how much I appreciated these efforts, please know it now.

Chapter 22

Angels and Music in the Dungeon

*Nothing ever succeeds which exuberant
spirits have not helped to produce.*
–Nietzsche

Now that radiation was complete, it was time to move on to the chemotherapy. Because of the radiation, my complexion had taken on a reddish-burnt hue, and I had diarrhea. There were to be two megadoses of chemo – the first, VP-16, and the second, cytoxan. I had never had VP-16 and had no idea what to expect or what side effects I would have, but I knew that I would soon find out.

The nurse, Regina, explained that my blood pressure must be continually monitored during the infusion of this drug, because it caused a decrease in blood pressure, and it could be dangerous if pressure dropped too low. I didn't like the idea of being hooked up to this machine with the nurse monitoring me from outside of the room; I wanted Regina to stay in the room with me in case something went wrong. I smiled because I knew that my angels would take care of the details. "Regina, I just want you to know that my angels are not going to let the machine work because I need you to stay in here with me." She smiled, disregarding me, and brought the blood pressure machine in and hooked it up. Since it is standard procedure to always test the equipment, she hooked it up on me, but it wouldn't work. She kept trying to get it to work but with no luck. She hooked it up on herself and it worked; then she'd hook it up to me and it wouldn't work. She found another machine. This machine she hooked up on herself first and it worked perfectly, so then she hooked it up to me and decided to watch it a few times. It worked the first time. Staring at her I told her that it wouldn't work anymore. Sure enough, it didn't work. Regina did the same series of tests on everyone in the room; it worked on everyone, including, her, but not on me. I smiled and winked and told them that my angels would not allow the machine to work because I wanted her to stay in the room with me.

I had one day of rest before receiving my megadose of Cytoxin. Finally my next to last dose of chemotherapy was administered. I was looking forward to this final dose because I knew that I would never have chemotherapy again. These doses of chemo were not the regular strong doses of chemo, they were megadoses of chemo. I understood them to be four times the standard dose.

With the Cytoxin, the VP-16, and all the radiation treatments, my body and mind were showing the effects of massive breakdown. I was throwing up so frequently that the nurses would not allow me any more food. They even took away my popsicles. The only food I received was through my IV bag. The worst of the side effects, I knew, were yet to come.

December 2, 1992, arrived, and I was feeling pretty tough but was very grateful that this was my transplant day. Dr. Blume was administering my transplant. My marrow had been divided, treated, and sterilized prior to its return to my system. The technicians had stored my white cells in DMSO. They were carefully frozen until they reached a temperature of -90 degrees C, and then they were stored in a freezer of liquid nitrogen until the day of their return, December 2, 1992. The cells were then slightly thawed to a slurpy consistency before being slowly injected to me via my IV catheter.

Dr. Blume liked to have music playing during the transplant and asked me to choose something I liked. I, who enjoy music, chose an instrumental tape called "Dreamflight." Dr. Blume, Jerry, and I were there. There were two bags of marrow to be returned. When Dr. Blume walked in, I already had the music playing. While he was listening to the music trying to determine whether or not it was appropriate, the nurse was bringing in hot blankets to cover me. After a moment he decided that the music would work and began the injection of my marrow slush. He prepared us for the smell of rotting seafood. My senses were all quite dull now, so fortunately for me, the smell was minimal. This was good! As the marrow was injected, my body became very cold and began shaking. The warm blankets were being layered and rotated one on top of another until you could hardly see me below all the blankets. After the marrow was returned it took a few hours before my body temperature warmed to a more comfortable level. For the next few days, I was safe from vampires. I smelled like garlic and rotten oysters.

Even though the transplant was complete, my body was still deteriorating. Sores were increasing by the minute in my mouth. I wasn't able to swallow and continuously drooled. I had a suction tube like dentists use next to my bed and every few minutes I'd have to vacuum the saliva and fluid draining from my mouth. Because of the VP-16, my skin was turning from burnt red to deep purple, as well as my body swelling many sizes beyond my normal size. My hands and feet were turning into claws and nubs, and I could hardly walk, stand, or hold a glass. It hurt to even hold the phone. The little bit of hair I had grown back from the last series of chemo injections began to fall out again. Every bit of urine and feces that exited my body was being checked and measured. Horrifying dreams and hallucinations of war and captivity filled my mind.

One night when the nurses' assistant came in to take the usual blood pressure, temperature, and abdominal measurement, I was so startled that I jumped. When I jumped, my tongue, which had been resting on the roof on my mouth, remained there, and a huge piece of my tongue and the roof of my mouth both tore. Alarmed, I buzzed the nurse and tried to tell her that my tongue had broken and that it was just hanging loose in my mouth. After examining me, she called a doctor.

He decided that it would be best not to remove the damaged tissue. The torn pieces of flesh had to remain in place to dry and fall off by themselves. If they cut the flesh off, there would be a loss of blood, which I couldn't afford to lose. It was the strangest sensation to not be able to see what was going on but to feel this loose piece of flesh in my mouth.

After a few days, this chunk did, indeed, dry up and drop off. I called the nurses and told them what had happened. I didn't think they believed me so I wrapped the flesh in a tissue and saved it for them. I remembered a friend calling to check on how I was doing, and I told her that my tongue had fallen off and that I saved it for the nurses. Now I realize that my tongue didn't actually fall off but a portion of the skin that had blistered did.

About eight times every day, I had to do mouth maintenance. No toothbrushes were used, only a sponge on a stick and swishing with different types of disgusting medicated mouthwashes. One morning I woke up and approached my sink to do my morning mouth care, and when I looked in the mirror, I saw two black eyes looking back at me. I started to cry; I didn't know what had happened. The doctors told me that because my platelet count was down I would bruise easily. I must have rubbed my eyes in the night and this alone had blackened them. The doctors, nurses, and Jerry told me not to cry or blow my nose because it would make them worse. In such a drugged and emotional state, all I could do was cry and blow my nose.

Even though, up until now, this whole process had seemed pretty gruesome, my skin was the worst part for me. It hurt and itched. I was swollen and purple from my head to the bottom of my feet. The blanket itself hurt if it touched my skin. My family took turns rubbing lotion into my arms and legs. The nurses and staff continually sent in different lotions, each one better than the last, all in hopes of relieving my discomfort. At the initial moment of contact the lotion seemed to help but after a few moments, discomfort returned.

The physical therapist would exercise my body because most of the time, I could hardly walk or move. In any case, I was restricted to my room because it was isolation time – I was quarantined in a sterile environment. Sometimes I was able to perform exercises in bed under the direction of the therapist, but there were moments when everything was impossible. Twice a day I had to use vaginal suppositories for the prevention of yeast infections because of all the antibiotics. I couldn't even insert the suppositories and had to have assistance with this as well as with taking a shower. Fortunately this helplessness lasted only a few days, but they were awful days. Prior to my brother's arrival there was a thirty-six hour interval that the doctors became concerned that I would not survive the transplant.

I was at my worst when my brother arrived late one evening. The nurse came in and told me that Glen, would be in shortly after he finished scrubbing. I had been so excited that he was coming because I didn't think he would show up, but now that he was here, I didn't want him to see me like this. I got up out of bed and held my door shut so he couldn't get in. Only after he talked to me for a few minutes would I let him in. I started crying as he helped me back to bed. He was smiling as he came through the door with a Christmas pillow and a stuffed cat.

Chapter 23

Calling All Crew Members

In the Pilgrimage of the Spirit, it is the strong and
steadfast aspiration to meet God face to face
that is the pathfinder, first and last.
—Dilip Kumar Roy, Pilgrim of the Stars

The nightmares became "daymares" and became increasingly worse. In most of my dreams, I would be held captive, unable to escape. The scenes usually took place in the aftermath of a nuclear holocaust. There was one dream I had during this time that had a different twist. Three time travelers had crashed in my room. When the first one crashed, we (meaning me and my guides) couldn't tell how to help it because its physiology was so different from ours. Then a second and a third crashed and by seeing and understanding what was wrong with the last two, we were able to figure out how to repair the first one. My time travelers needed supplies, equipment, and a place to rest. While still dreaming, I apparently got up, actually removed the blanket and sheets from my bed, and began moving the furniture in the room (this was during the time that my hands were like claws). I was dividing everything up in my room for the time travelers, and I had just begun to try to figure out how to get my IV pole to them since they needed this too. During this brief deliberation, and in the process of reaching up to remove my IV bags, one of my nurses, Susie, came in to find out what all the noise was. I explained to her that I must do this because these time travelers had crashed in my room and needed my help. Susie said, "Beth, I'll take care of your time travelers; you go back to bed now." I smiled and said okay.

After that I would no longer use the hospital blanket because it hurt my skin; instead I used a really soft red afghan that had been given to me at my party. Most of the pajamas and clothing that I had chosen were of softer colors because of their soothing qualities. I intentionally did not bring any red clothing because red is a stimulating color and could aggravate my fever and inflammation. However, this red blanket was the softest and warmest ever, and it was a gift from friends. I just made sure that it didn't directly touch my skin.

Every night or "day" a newer version of my dreams would emerge. For example, in one dream, I was walking down a dark highway with someone and there was road kill everywhere. I was looking for a house that had not been destroyed by nuclear weapons so that I could take a shower and clean up. The only place open was a convenience store where I had to stand in line. When I got to the counter, all they had were cookies, candy and sodas, none of which I wanted. The darkness in my dreams was like a night without a moon or stars. I knew that this blackness represented the flickering of my soul as it tried to gain ground and stabilize.

Chapter 24

Escape and Release

*Love cures people – both the ones who give it
and the ones who receive it.*
–Dr. Karl Menninger

When the doctors came in the middle of the night, I began chewing them out for moving me while I was sleeping. I just knew that they had moved me, which they hadn't, but I refused to sleep for three nights. I decided that I needed to stay awake so I could prevent them from moving me again. Now, every time the doctors came in, I had something to say like "You don't know what you're doing," and "I'm not going to just lie here." The drugs had taken a toll on my body and mind; chaos and destruction filled my thoughts and dreams.

One night, a German doctor that we called Dr. Klaus because no one could pronounce his last name had come in to see how I was doing and to perform my nightly examination. I refused to allow him to touch me and threw him out of my room. Dr. Long was sent in to complete the task. He started out slowly, just talking with me, and then asked if it would be okay if he examined me. "Okay," I agreed. I didn't remember this incident, but the next day when all the doctors came in for their usual visit, Dr. Klaus just colored on my poster. Dr. Long laughed while refreshing my memory about the night before. After a few days of this behavior, I asked why Dr. Klaus was always coloring, and he just smiled and told me that his job was to color.

During all my delusions and nightmares, I had another dream of being held prisoner. The dream was so vivid. I was tied to a couple's bed in the basement. Once in a while they would check on me. I had to get out. During my break-out attempt, I actually blasted out of my isolation room while I was still sleeping. Considering the condition of my body, it was quite a feat for me to even get the door open. When I came out of the room an assistant nurse just looked at me and reported to someone that I was out. When the doctors came the next day, I told Dr. Long that I had to get out of my room because I was disoriented and didn't know where I was. I knew that my white blood cell count was not where it was supposed to be, but I pleaded, "Please, let me out." He consented to letting me leave my room and walk around the unit a couple of times. Instead of leaving my room once and walking twice around the CHU floor, I would leave my room twice and walk once around each time.

My favorite nurse, Susie, was taking a week off at Christmas, so when she came in to say good-bye for the holidays, she brought me a Christmas gift sack with a green knit cap and some Kool-aid inside. I had been wearing an old yellow cap to keep my head warm; the green one was a welcomed change. I never got to see Susie again.

Everyone was so very thoughtful at putting their best foot forward in an effort to comfort and support me. My body was trying to repair itself, but it was a long road. A few days after Dr. Long gave me permission to leave my room, my white blood cell count went up. The doctors had originally needed these numbers before the isolation could be lifted. Now I had formal permission to leave my room and to do so more frequently, but I had to remain on the CHU floor. My appetite had returned earlier than was expected, and I was eating more each day. In addition, I was

118

continually harassing the staff to provide root-beer popsicles. My purple swollen skin had begun peeling in huge chunks of multiple skin layers. Sometimes I would spend the entire day peeling skin. At one point, I peeled skin off my heel that was so thick it looked like a wax mold. The good side to this very expensive chemical peel was that I had no more calluses.

Now that I was out of isolation and improving daily, I was moved to a room across the hall which I shared with another woman for the last few days of my stay. She was a nice lady and we would talk some, but pretty much we each had our focus on our own healing process. The only difficult part about sharing was the use of one bathroom where every excrement had to be measured. The smell got pretty bad. She was just beginning her hospital stay and I was leaving, I hoped. I don't even remember her name, but when I left, I wished her a quick, painless recovery with many blessings.

After much pleading, it was decided on December 22nd that because of my swift healing progress, I would be permitted to check out of the hospital on Christmas Eve day. This didn't mean I would be going home to Reno, but that I would move into H.O.M.E., an apartment complex on the hospital grounds for the transplant patients. I hadn't seen a friend or family member in a couple of days, so I was really looking forward to my mother's arrival on the 23rd of December. The office that handled admissions into the apartment would be closing at 4:00 p.m. on the 23rd and would not be reopening until the day after Christmas.

My mother was going to have to fly into San Jose, rent a car, drive to Palo Alto (which wasn't very far), and find the admissions office for the apartments and make sure that I was checked in so that I could move the next day. My anxiety was high and the "what-if" attacks were very much like panic attacks. I believe those were the closest things

I've ever had to panic attacks. My heart was racing and many different fears came up – like, she'd miss the plane, get lost, have a wreck, or arrive at the office after it closed. I wanted out of that hospital more than anything. I began pacing the halls, back and forth. Then I went into Angela's office (the head staff nurse) and began bawling hysterically. It felt like weeks went by before my mother got to the hospital. When she finally arrived, she informed me that everything had been completed in record time. She had gotten to the office about thirty minutes before they closed. I was so excited; I could leave, but the doctors said I'd have to wait until around noon on Christmas Eve.

My mother stayed in the hospital with me that evening for a few hours and then left so she could get to the grocery store for food. Even though the apartment was already clean, according to Momma, it wasn't clean enough for me, so she stayed up till 4:00 a.m. cleaning so everything would be ready for me to move in the next day. While Momma was shopping and cleaning, I was packing. I left out only what I would need for the next morning. I told Regina that any tests that needed to be done should be scheduled for this evening or first thing in the morning, because at straight up noon I was getting out. I think Regina was glad when I left because I was pestering her every few minutes asking about this or that to make sure I could leave. After I packed, I paced the floors. When the doctors came in that night, I told them that Dr. Blume had told me that I could leave. I told them that they were to make sure that I was their first stop in the morning so I wouldn't be held up. They teased me for a while but then said that I could be their first stop. Dr. Klaus wanted to know where his colored markers and picture were. I just smiled and told him that there would be no more coloring – the markers and poster were packed, and I was getting out.

Chapter 25

Santa Came Early

*If the only prayer you say in your life is
"Thank You," that would suffice.*
—Meister Eckhart

Every single day in the hospital, I had received letters, cards, boxes, and caring phone calls. Everyone commented on how much support I received. Some of the nurses would joke and say that they were going to pass some of my mail around to other patients. All I can say is thank you, thank you, thank you to all the staff, my family, my friends, and their friends who wrote me and sent me wonderful little surprises filled with hope and love during my stay at the hospital. I have a cup that I received while in the hospital, and I still don't know who sent it. No one seems to know who sent it!

The morning I checked out, the physical therapist came in and took me into the main part of the hospital. He worked with me on climbing stairs, and he explained to me the need to take it easy and not get too exhausted. I was extremely weak after my ordeal. Simple things that I had taken for granted now served as a reminder to me to give thanks and gratitude. After having me climb the stairs, the physical therapist continued to show me other exercises that would strengthen my body.

I had diarrhea that day, but I was afraid to tell anyone because I thought they wouldn't let me leave. After messing myself three times, I asked the nurse when she came in if I could have something for diarrhea. (I was so embarrassed.) Yes, I got the medication, and, YES, I was permitted to leave, but not until "one" last thing. "One" included chest x-rays, blood tests, and the inhalation of some medication to prevent pneumonia. By the time I got out on Christmas Eve, it was just a few minutes past noon. The doctors had loaded me up with prescriptions of every kind. I was given a list of *do's* and *don'ts* on a daily basis, a weekly basis, a monthly basis and a yearly basis. I was surprised that this was to continue so long after I got out of the hospital, but nonetheless I had my list of restrictions that lasted one year. Even though I was worrying about yesterday and tomorrow, I tried to stay focused on today, but between the side effects from the medications I was taking, and the withdrawals I was going through from stopping the heavier medications, it was hard to stay calm and focused.

Because of all the medications, my body was more toxic than it had ever been, probably more like radioactive; I think it glowed in the dark. I was happy to be getting out, but I was depressed, hyperactive, and cried a lot. I knew my moods could be attributed to the drugs. I told my mother that I wanted to go to the mall, an outdoor mall, and walk around. I had been cooped up for too long. Momma said she thought it would be too much and I shouldn't tire myself but she would ask the nurse if it would be okay. Regina told Momma that it would be fine and good for me. Actually she said, *"Please* take her for a walk." As I was leaving the hospital, I saw Dr. Blume. I ran up to him and told him thank you and that I was leaving. He looked at me and smiled and said, "Who said you could leave?" I responded with, "You did!" and then hugged him and left to go to my apartment.

Chapter 26

Grateful for Love

There is a land of the living and a land
of the dead and the bridge is love. . . .
—Thornton Wilder

There was a lot to unload from the car since I had taken so much to the hospital, but the complex had carts which made moving much easier. Momma got everything unloaded and brought it upstairs. It was a cute little apartment – one bedroom and bath with a living area and kitchen. The management office had placed a small Christmas tree with lights and bows on the dining table. It was cute, but I couldn't have any plants around me so Momma put the tree outside on the back porch. I would look at the Christmas tree through the sliding glass door. After we unpacked, we went to the Stanford Mall nearby and walked around for a few minutes. A horde of people were all trying to do last-minute Christmas shopping. I loved the Disney store because of the colors and because everyone was so happy. My watch had quit working while I was in the hospital, so I bought a Minnie Mouse watch for my self as a Christmas present and immediately put on in the store. I had a huge smile on my face, but no one could see it because of the mask. Anytime I left the apartment I had to wear a mask that had been designed to protect the wearer from asbestos dust particles at construction sites, but for me the purpose of wearing this heavy-duty mask was to keep germs out.

Now that I had had my little excursion, and some of my anxious energy had worn off, it was time to go H.O.M.E. I was hungry! Food tastes so much better out of the hospital. Momma had been given a copy of my *do's* and *don'ts* food list the night before so she could do some grocery shopping. My list was limited; it mostly consisted of well-cooked meats and canned foods because they were supposedly more sterile. Pretty much anything outside of hospital food smelled and tasted great. When we returned to the apartment, Momma fixed me lamb stew. She was concerned that it would be bland because I was permitted to have only mild cooked seasonings and absolutely no spicy seasonings. During her shopping, she had found a mild seasoning blend that was great. The smell of the food cooking was the best, and my palate wanted meat and more meat. This was the first meal after too much hospital food, and it was great! I ate as much as my stomach could hold, which wasn't much.

After my wonderful meal I began cleaning out my purse, and in my wallet I found a worn silver cross. Where had it come from? It looked like the cross my grandfather had carried for thirty or more years. Did Momma recognize the cross? She confirmed that it was Pap's. I called Pap and asked him when he had given it to me. He said that right before they had returned to Dallas, he put the cross in my Christmas card. I was extremely moved and honored that he would give me his cross, and in my change purse it remains to this day.

Chapter 27

Support Through Withdrawals

When I planted my pain in the field of patience
it bore fruit of happiness.
—Kahlil Gibran

Momma had brought presents for me and arranged them by the sliding glass doors close to where the Christmas tree stood outside. The phone never stopped ringing. Family, friends and even people I didn't know called offering support and prayers while wishing me happy holidays. Each one offered a toast that it was the best Christmas present ever to have me out of the hospital. My emotions were mixed, and I was full of hope and fear, mostly because of all the drugs in my system. It had begun raining and I found myself crying as I watched the rain fall off the eaves onto the little Christmas tree. The poor little tree kept falling over, and Momma would go out in the rain to stand it back up.

Earlier in the evening Momma had begun prepping food for our Christmas dinner. She had bought some chicken breasts, but when she opened the chicken, the smell told her it was bad. And here it was 5:00 p.m. on Christmas Eve. She called the grocery store where she had bought the chicken and explained that the chicken breasts were to be part of our Christmas meal and that I had just gotten out of the hospital. The girl at the store was extremely nice and hand-delivered a replacement package of chicken. Our Christmas dinner was baked chicken and canned asparagus. We laughed at the limp asparagus. I think that was the only time I ever ate canned asparagus. We decided it wouldn't be part of our regular diet. Dessert was canned peaches. This canned diet that the hospital wanted me to follow really sucked, especially since I had been eating fresh food for years. My appetite was increasing with each meal. I was always hungry, and if I wasn't eating a meal, I was snacking.

My spirit was restless as it worked on being put back together. That night it seemed sleep would never come, and I found myself pacing the floor in hopes of getting sleepy. For now, the recliner seemed more comfortable than the hard bed, and I was able to drift in and out of sleep. I put a movie in the VCR and listened to the rain as it began to fall. The sound of water gently falling finally lulled my body and mind to sleep.

Christmas morning. I didn't have to go to the hospital. This was the first day without any doctors, testing or hospitals. Yea! Momma had set out a Christmas stocking and a few more gifts. I was upset that I didn't have anything for my mother – or for anyone else, for that matter. No one seemed to notice or care; society's rules didn't apply today. Everyone was wishing me a very merry Christmas. I thought the phone had rung a lot before, but today I needed a headset because all I did was hold the phone and talk. There was one call after another.

I enjoyed talking to everyone, even though I got tired just holding the phone. Some of the medication made me nervous, so I walked up and down the stairwells to burn off the energy while building up my strength at the same time. Nothing was open; otherwise, I would have gone to the mall. As I walked, Momma continued to prepare for a festive Christmas. She had bought red plates and green napkins to brighten up the day and the meal. She worked hard to make every moment special.

Jerry called when he got off work that evening. I was so happy to hear from him – I always waited eagerly for his calls. Sometimes I couldn't wait, and I would often awaken him by my calls in the middle of night when I was pacing the floors. I wanted to go home. Jerry would put my animals on the phone, and I would assure them that I would be home soon. I was most concerned about Sylvester. He was my thirteen-year-old cat, and I had had him since he was a kitten. I adopted him from the S.P.C.A. in Dallas. I never even named him until I took him in to be neutered. The vet asked me what his name was and I looked at this black and white long-haired cat and said, "Sylvester." I would have dreams about him while I was in the hospital and would sometimes see him staring at me in my room.

I wanted to go home yesterday. But the nurses and doctors said that it might not be until around the end of January or the first of February before I could go home, and only if all went well. It was hard to predict. I wanted my husband, my home, my animals, and my life back. I wanted to rediscover what normal was all about.

The week between Christmas and New Year's Jerry had to work, and many of those days he worked twelve-hour shifts. I heard from him every day, but he was tired and wouldn't talk long. Up until now we had talked on the phone two and three times a day, and of course, he had been at the hospital each week for two or three days. I remember one day in the hospital when he helped me walk around the unit. He didn't have to wear his mask outside of my room, but I had to wear mine. He was kissing me on the neck, telling me that when we got back to the room where he had to wear a mask and I didn't, it would be my turn to kiss him. We laughed and enjoyed the moment. I missed him so much.

The day after Christmas, my Grandma Ruby, Aunt Shirley, and Aunt Irene stopped in for a short visit. My mother kept getting up, and going out of the room. I couldn't figure out what she was doing, so I asked her to come sit down. After she sat down, I excused myself and went into the bathroom, and when I sat down on the toilet seat, it was wet with alcohol. Every time someone used the bathroom, Momma had been jumping up and wiping the bathroom down with alcohol. She was great at keeping the germs away.

After our visitors left, I had to return to the hospital for another blood transfusion. Until my blood counts stayed where the doctors wanted them, I had to continue getting blood or plasma transfusions. There was another young woman there who was having another type of chemo treatment for those who didn't qualify for the transplant. Her name was Utah and her husband had been able to take a long vacation to be with her all of the time. He helped feed her and showed her great love and admiration. He was so tender. It made me miss Jerry even more and I felt lonely. Jerry had no vacation time available, but he would come down every week for a day or two. I wanted to go home!

A few days later, I went to the hospital for more blood work and x-rays. My blood was holding strong, and I didn't have to receive any more transfusions. I was so glad, but now it was time to move on to the next step. For me, the next step was taking out my catheter, but Dr. Long said "no" and that I should wait for a few more days to make sure that my blood maintained its count. Even though I understood, I was disappointed. I knew that I would go home soon, and every day I pushed the doctors to let me do more and to go home. I felt like Dorothy in the Wizard of Oz. There's no place like home!

Chapter 28

Understanding

Those who wish to sing always find a song.
—Swedish Proverb

A few days after I got out of the hospital, I went to the grocery store with my mother. She dropped me off at the door and then went to park the car. There was a bold man coming out of the store who also had a heavy-duty asbestos protection mask on. I knew that he, too, was a transplant survivor. He saw me, and his eyes lit up, and he just started talking to me like we were old friends who hadn't seen each other in years. I don't even remember what we said, but there was a camaraderie between us. As I told Dr. Forsythe later, "I've done my tour of duty, thank you." This man and I had both done our tour of duty, and even though the battle fields were different, we knew the strength it took to withstand against all odds.

While I was out, I would overhear people talking, trying to guess what my condition might be and why I was wearing a mask. No one would ever ask me. I would have preferred that they ask and not just stare and talk as though I didn't hear them. I was self-conscious about my appearance. I still had my black eyes; they were not healing very quickly. I had to wear this mask, and, for the time being, had to wear my glasses instead of my contacts.

My sister arrived the night before my mother left. The "guards" had changed shifts, and Debbie was now staying at the apartment helping me. Every day I wanted to go to the mall to walk around and especially to go to the Disney Store. Over and over again, I would go in just to feel the colors and the happiness of the store, and the store employees were beginning to remember me. Debbie wanted to buy me some more scarves, so we stopped in a scarf and tie shop. My vision was poor and limited because of the mask, and my glasses were not the correct prescription. Out of the corner of my eye, I was looking at this beautifully sculpted black mannequin behind me. His features were perfect and he was well-dressed in a GQ sort of way. I just kept admiring it. He then made a slight move, and I screamed and jumped. Everyone in the store jumped, including him. I apologized and explained that his features were gorgeous and I thought he was a mannequin. He said "Thank you," and that he had never been called a mannequin before!

Chapter 29

Taking Care of the Details

*The future belongs to those who believe
in the beauty of their dreams.*
—Eleanor Roosevelt

The day before Debbie arrived, Momma had taken me to the hospital for another checkup and to determine if my catheter could be removed. Jerry would be arriving any minute. Dr. Long and Dr. Blume gave me the go ahead to return home to Reno. They felt that any further follow ups could be done by Dr. Forsythe. Just moments before my catheter was to be removed, Jerry walked into the room. I was so excited that I immediately blurted out "Jerry, I can go home!" as he walked in. Saturday, January 9, 1993, would be my day of freedom! He didn't seem as excited as I was. He wanted me to stay a week longer because the roads to Reno had been closed most of the winter due to heavy snowfall. He didn't know how he was going to get the house ready in time. There had to be all kinds of spring cleaning before I could enter the house. I was upset thinking that Jerry didn't want me to come home, and I wanted more than anything to go home and have a normal life. The date that I had been waiting for was only a few days away.

Yes! Now was the time to remove my catheter. It had been a great friend by saving my veins from the agony of daily needle punctures, but I had felt like a monster from the moment it was put in. I had heard that the doctors just yank it out of your chest when it's time to remove it, and part of me was nervous. When the doctor came in, I asked if this was true. "Yes, but it's more of a gentle yank and pull," he told me. After I took a deep breath and relaxed a moment, he pressed one hand on my upper chest where the catheter was inserted into my artery and with the other hand holding on to the exposed end, pulled with a strong, steady tug. I could feel my artery being pulled from the inside, and my body began to shake. Both my physical and spiritual bodies on the energetic grid felt thrown off balance (not that it was in balance in the first place). As I was shaking, my body became cold; out came the hot blankets to warm me up. Another tug and the catheter was out. Dr. Martinez applied pressure to stop the bleeding and asked the nurse to hand him a twenty-pound sand bag, which he placed on my chest for twenty minutes to guarantee blood clotting.

Jerry stayed that night and then flew back to Reno absolutely crazy with trying to figure out how to both work and clean the house. He had left my car with Debbie and me so we could get around and drive back home. I told him to call a few of my friends and ask if they would come over and help, which they did. That took a lot of pressure off him, but he still wanted me to stay another week. I was hysterical and told him that I was coming home even if I had to drive myself.

The next three days seemed so long as each morning and night I watched the weather and listened to road conditions. Every night there were hours when the roads over the mountains were closed. It was Friday night, I wanted to get back home, and I knew that Saturday was my best shot before another storm hit. My sister hadn't driven much in snow, especially not this much snow; she wasn't used to mountain roads, and I didn't feel safe with her driving. She tried to convince me that she could drive just fine in heavy snow, but I wasn't buying it. I called Jerry and told him that I was coming home and that he needed to fly down and drive me back home. He was flustered and on edge, but he finally agreed to fly down. He called the airlines and then called me back. He was landing at 8:00 a.m. Saturday, and Debbie and I were to pick him up at the airport and then he would drive us home.

Early Saturday morning, Debbie and I began hauling all my stuff down to the car, but because everyone had sent me so much, we couldn't get all of it in; we had to save room for the three of us. No matter what we tried, it wasn't going to fit. The things that meant the most we packed. The stuff that didn't really matter I left in the apartment for the next person. It was time to go, and I said my good-byes. I was excited and scared. As a matter of fact, I was scared of everything. I was thinking that the plane might crash while Jerry was on it or we'd get in a car wreck while driving back home. My mind just kept thinking of any tragic event that could possibly occur. I was going through withdrawals from the numerous drugs and wanted my life to be normal. My mind was cluttered and in a panic. I just tried to keep my focus on getting home and getting stronger and having a normal life. My mind drifted as I dreamt of sitting on the front porch, sipping some hot herbal tea. *"Dull"* was looking pretty good right now.

Chapter 30

Coming Home

As to me, I know of nothing else but miracles.
-Walt Whitman

Debbie and I arrived at the airport on time, and within a few minutes, Jerry came out the doors and towards the car. What an emotional time – I was going home! Jerry was a good driver and had driven in a lot of snow, especially over these mountains. Over the last couple of months, he probably had driven over them a dozen or more times. There was no doubt he knew the road.

Even though both radio and television broadcasts stated that the road conditions were good and that the road over the mountains would be open, we wouldn't know for certain until we got to the pass. Just east of Sacramento on I-80 cars were backed up, but within minutes they began letting cars through; that was a good sign. Farther into the mountains there was another roadblock. Everyone's tires were being checked to see if they would make it through the snow. For miles cars were pulled over as "men for hire" in their orange jumpsuits put chains on the tires. We had chains in the trunk just in case we needed them, but luckily, our tires passed the inspection. We pushed forward through the pass. The snow towered over us except where the two tire tracks ran. This was the same winter that, just a week before, a young couple with their little baby were lost in the snow. As we stopped at a rest stop to use the restrooms, the snow was piled all the way up to the roof top. I told my sister, "See all this snow. Normally this rest stop had a pretty little pond in back of the building, but the snow had buried it." The snow looked so pretty – it definitely brightened up the cold.

We made incredible time considering the weather conditions. We made it back to Reno in four and a half hours, which was the normal amount of time if the roads were clear. When we arrived, my girlfriend Cathy, was trying to do the last little bit of cleaning. It felt great to be home, and it also felt sad. I thought the sadness had to do with all the restrictions that I had to follow for the next year.

Tired, I still wanted to walk through my house and just look. Maybe I wanted to see if everything was the same or if anything was different. Afterwards I sat on the couch and visited with Cathy for a little bit. Sylvester came out but refused to acknowledge me and jumped into my sister's lap and cuddled with her. I was hurt, but I wasn't allowed to pet him anyway because of germs. That entire evening Sylvester would have nothing to do with me; he wouldn't even look at me. The next morning, my sister told me that as soon as I went to bed, Sylvester jumped down and didn't pay her any further attention. He had done that only to show me how mad and hurt he was. As I walked down the hall, he came up and bit me on the ankle. Sylvester had been with me for so many years, I had to find a way to satisfy both our needs. I decided that I would wrap him in a towel and hold him, so for the next two to three months I held and petted him in the towel.

Everything I did had restrictions of some kind. Some limitations lasted for ninety days, some for six months and other things not for one year. I couldn't do many things that most people took for granted. For instance, I couldn't check the soil in my house plants to see if they needed watering, and I couldn't eat leftovers that were more than 24 hours old.

I couldn't even leave the house without wearing my heavy duty mask. As stated in the post-transplant handouts, we needed to purchase an air filtering system. I definitely agreed with this restriction because the winter air quality in Reno was always bad. Because of the air quality, I was advised not to walk, and I definitely couldn't go swimming for many, many months, so I bought a cross-country-ski glider and Jane Fonda's exercise video tape and step. I exercised in my own home with my air purifiers. We had to sell our aquariums because I couldn't clean fish tanks for the next year.

All I wanted to do was to be normal and to do the things that I had done before, so instead of complaining any longer, I decided to do the things that I could do. I started catching up on some sewing projects, and reading some books that I hadn't had time for before. Naps became a daily event, usually in the late afternoon, and as different restrictions were lifted I would add new activities to my day. Now that I was home, I began adding fresher foods back into my diet. So many parts of my body had limitations in general functioning. My nose couldn't smell, my eyes struggled to focus, and my taste buds were diminished, but I hoped daily that all these functions would return sooner, rather than later.

Debbie stayed for a week and went through my entire house double-checking my friend's cleaning. If it wasn't satisfactory, she'd redo it. One of her projects was cleaning and relining my cabinet shelves. She kept food on the table, chauffeured me to my doctor, and kept me company. I found out that she, my brother, and stepfather had all pitched in to pay for my sister, Becky's, trip to Reno since she had the last shift. As much as I love Becky, it was definitely good that she was last, because I had more energy than she did and wound up doing most of the cooking and driving. I wasn't supposed to do any type of cleaning whatsoever, whether it be vacuuming, dusting, washing dishes, or scrubbing floors. As a matter of fact, I wasn't even supposed to be in the room when this was going on. I also couldn't walk down a detergent aisle at the grocery store. I actually didn't mind getting out of cleaning for a month or so, but out of habit, I would catch myself wiping a counter here and there. I did miss not being able to pick up or play with my animals or plants.

Chapter 31

Temporary Setbacks

Avoiding danger is no safer in the long run than outright exposure.
Life is either a daring adventure or nothing.
—Helen Keller

Sherrie came to my house for my first few counseling sessions with her until I had the strength to meet her at her office. Because of all of the restrictions on my daily activities, within a month of being home from the hospital, I was beginning to get bored. I suggested to both Sherrie and Jerry that maybe I could go back to work part-time. Neither of them thought this was a good idea, but I wanted a trial run. My employer, John Clarkston, had been calling me, wondering when I could return. After convincing Dr. Forsythe that if I got too tired with a few hours a week I would take further time off, I called John and informed him of the stipulations. He agreed, and thirty days after I came home from Stanford, I returned to work.

During the first three weeks, I had a cold along with the flu for the entire time. I was tired all the time. After returning from lunch one day, John told me that I looked yellow. Sure enough I did, so I headed for the doctor's office. Test results revealed that I had been exposed to hepatitis from one of the many blood transfusions, and I had to immediately stop working for another thirty days. Jerry had to have a shot to prevent him from contracting the hepatitis.

One week after my forced retirement, I developed a

rash, and the rash turned into shingles. All across my stomach and back I had huge pus-filled blisters. I had never had shingles, and they were painful. Once I realized what I had, I thought I could take care of them myself, but they were out of control. My body was just too weak and broken down. Dr. Forsythe said that this was the worst case of shingles that he had ever seen, and he gave me a prescription for Zovirax both in cream and pill form.

Both the Stanford doctors and Dr. Forsythe wanted me to take only a daily multiple vitamin because they said that they wanted my body to heal and return to normal on its own. At first, I thought this was a good idea, but now I questioned it. My body didn't have a clue what normal was; I had been on chemo for four years and had just gone through a bone-marrow transplant. I called Dr. Forsythe and informed him that I was going to take control of what my body needed nutritionally. I felt that their approach wasn't working and that I knew more about vitamins, herbs, and food than they did. Dr. Forsythe didn't argue; actually, he agreed with me. I started taking the multiple vitamin, plus multi-minerals, vitamins C and E, beta carotene, Barley Green, Dr. Donsbach's magnesium oxide and a high stress B-complex along with B-12 injections. I also took colloidal silver to ward off infection. Plus, I was eating healthier. Herbally, I used Jason Winter's tea, chamomile, ginger root, echinacea, and more.

Next, I called up the psychic surgeon and made a private appointment. Within that session and during the hours that followed, the shingles began drying and disappearing before my eyes. I was beginning to have some sense that my health was returning.

My senses were improving in tiny increments but were still very numb. I was sad that when Jerry and I made love I felt nothing in my left breast, and my loins were just as numb. I began going through menopause, which included experiencing hot flashes. Both the chemotherapy and radiation from the transplant had truly stopped my menses and numbed my senses. I had hoped that my angels had protected my reproductive system, but it was *my* life that needed to be helped, not that of a future unconceived child. My reproductive system was just one area that I had to work on to regain circulation so I could feel the energy move through. I called Tanzy, my Hellerwork practitioner, and set up a few sessions. Intuitively, I knew that the bodywork would release the trauma and return the sensations. In addition, I increased circulation to these areas by cupping my hands and slapping the entire torso region.

One thing I was becoming increasingly aware of was that the dreams of being in school had ended. The classroom dream scenes were now replaced nightly with dreams of traveling and moving. These dreams seemed to be a necessary part of reclaiming my life and health. Even spirits were stopping by to give the thumbs-up sign and to hang out for a while. Until now I didn't realize that through all these years, I had been honing my intuition. It was all a very natural progression so I could stay alive.

After one of my visits with Sherrie, she suggested that Jerry and I might have a few things to discuss and work on. We had lived our entire marriage to date in survival mode. I knew she was probably right, but for the time being, we were doing well. Each day I was getting stronger, and I was now able to maintain a twenty-hour work week without tiring. Jerry began working extra hours so we could catch up on our expenses. It seemed that "normal" was on its way, or so I hoped.

Chapter 32

The Power of Believing

The mind has the power to affect groups of atoms,
and even tamper with the odds of atomic behavior;
and that even the course of the world is not
predetermined by physical laws, but may be altered
by the uncaused, or CAUSED, volition of human being."
–Dr. A. S. Eddington, Physicist

Few men have imagination enough for reality.
–Johann Wolfgang von Goethe

Part of my daily routine, as prescribed by the doctors, was to take notice of any symptoms such as night sweats, swollen areas, low-grade fevers, weight loss, and loss of appetite. It had become natural over the years always to be poking around on myself checking for tumors. My appointments with Dr. Forsythe had been reduced from weekly to bi-monthly, and I was going in for another check up and blood test.

One day, after stepping out of the shower, I began drying myself off while unconsciously checking my body for tumors. There it was – one about the size of a thumb nail on my back. I completely freaked! I had just gone through a transplant! *No, this can't be happening. I'm not going to accept it.* My body trembled as I cried hysterically. God was always my prime target. Shaking my fist at the ceiling, I began screaming that, by God, I have done my tour of duty, and I am off the battlefields. I demanded that this be removed, now. Jerry came running in, and he began crying with me. He said Dr. Forsythe must be told when I went in for my appointment that day. I laid into him, making him swear not to say a word, and I said I would take care of it myself later. After much convincing, he agreed that he wouldn't say anything for now, but if it wasn't gone before my next appointment, he would tell Dr. Forsythe himself.

I made a promise to the heavens to move on to wherever my higher path led me as long as this tumor disappeared. Jerry and I arrived at the doctor's office, and Jerry kept his promise. As I entered the waiting room, I prayed that the lump would disappear. It was never discovered. This event encouraged me further. I told my doctor that I was no longer looking for tumors, because if I was always looking, I would always find them. I decided that what I would look for from now on would be happier things. He agreed yet asked me to keep a look out. I agreed and left. The power of the mind to create is beyond our imagination!

When Jerry and I returned to the house, the tumor had truly disappeared! I knelt and gave my thanks of gratitude and kept my promise by beginning a stronger regimen of strengthening and cleansing my body. I tightened my diet by eliminating meat, cheese, bread, and sugar or any white by-products, while adding more blood purifying teas, fresh juices (carrot, beet, parsley), and increasing my raw food intake to eighty percent. Exercise became a daily practice instead of a three-or-four-times-a-week event. Books to strengthen my spirit became my daily practice. And I called friends that I knew would encourage and support me.

Chapter 33

As One Door Closes

In the middle of difficulty lies opportunity.
—Albert Einstein

Jerry had been putting in so many hours for so long with his work and with taking care of me that when his brothers called asking if he would come down and visit, I encouraged him to go, have fun, and relax. I knew that I was much stronger and would be just fine so in June, 1993, he flew back to Texas for a week of fishing. He seemed almost afraid to leave, and at the same time he wanted to go. He had been on call for almost seven years. Twice a day while he was gone he called to check on me; I was fine. Even though he had a good time with his brothers, he was relieved to come home.

The day after his return, he told me that he didn't think I needed him anymore. I reaffirmed my I love for him and agreed that I didn't need him the same way that I had, but said that that didn't mean we couldn't continue on our paths together. By mid-July his personality began changing. He started drinking coffee and smoking cigars, and when I would ask about these sudden changes, he would say that he had always drunk coffee and smoked cigars. Instead of coming home after work, he was going out and returning only after I went to bed. As his mannerisms, habits and activities changed, I became suspicious. I began dreaming that our relationship was ending and that he was involved with another woman, a friend of ours, but I couldn't tell with whom.

One day while wiping a counter, my hand hit his father's gold watch, which went flying. The crystal covering broke in the form of a triangle with a crack running through the three and six. My stomach turned in a knot at the sight of the triangle. Also, I knew that the number six represented family and home. The glass in the cabinet door of my antique desk also broke in the form of a triangle. Lots of things were falling and breaking in the form of a triangle. The combination of my dreams of him seeing another woman and glass breaking around me in the shape of triangles convinced me that he was having an affair. I had learned over the years to pay attention to the subtle messages.

If I invited friends over for dinner or just to visit, half the time he'd show up late. One night a good friend of ours had come over to visit. I had tried to prepare her in advance by telling her how he'd changed. She was shocked when she saw him, and after he walked out of the room, she turned to me and asked who this person was. I told her I didn't have a clue, but I wanted to know what had happened to the Jerry I knew! For a short period of time I thought he might be returning because of a brief turn-around while we were on vacation in San Diego. I made a promise that I would begin doing more and more things that I had always wanted to do, and one of them was to take a trip to the San Diego Zoo. Jerry and I spent five days in San Diego and had a blast. During this trip he agreed that marriage counseling would be a good idea, and when we returned I began looking into who would be a good counselor for us. My friend Sherri referred me to a psychologist named Chuck Holt. I trusted her and respected her opinion, so I made an appointment for Jerry and me.

The night before we were to go to the marriage counselor for our first appointment I had a dream.

Jerry had taken off, and I was in search of him. A friend said she would help me find him, so we got in a Suburban that drove on the railroad tracks. The tracks became a winding path down into some caves. As I went running through the caves, I saw that they were filled with men who were lost. Their souls didn't seem to be in their bodies, and their bodies were only shells. I stopped and asked if anyone had seen Jerry, and one man told me that he had gone deeper down and around a corner. When I ran around the corner there was a man with gray hair leaning on the post. He didn't even look up but just stood with his arms crossed. paused for just a moment before I saw Jerry behind the pillar. I screamed at him and punched him in the nose. It didn't phase him; he was much too numb or dead, but I felt bad and gently wiped the blood from his nose. The older man behind me never looked up, but said, "I think it's time to go home now." Then I woke up.

Chuck Holt came out to the waiting room to greet us, and this was when I realized that this was the same gray-haired man from my dream. Identical, except that Chuck wore glasses. He directed us into his office and offered us something to drink. He asked us questions and then listened to our responses. In a wise but non-abrasive way, he tried to help us. After each session, he would send us home with homework or something to think about for the week. Jerry and I had agreed to see him weekly until our problems were resolved. It took me about two weeks to finish the first homework assignment, which was mostly completing charts and answering questions about family and relationships.

Jerry never seemed to get the work done and he started rebelling about going in for our appointments. Every time he did go in, he would just repeat that he loved me and that I was beautiful but that he didn't think he was in love with me anymore. Jerry wouldn't agree to any homework that might improve our relationship, and he further distanced himself.

At what turned out to be our next-to-last session, Chuck Holt explained that we were going through post-traumatic stress syndrome. Basically, the war was over, and each of us was getting back to normal at different paces. Jerry wound up leaving the session early and threatened never to return. I stayed and cried while Chuck further explained that when young men are sent to war they become very responsible, but when they come home, they are just kids. The war was over, and Jerry had returned to being the kid he was before we met. Our whole marriage had definitely been a war zone with my cancer experience always hanging over our heads and consuming our lives.

Over the next week I began questioning Jerry about all of his overtime. I didn't believe that he was working. One morning my gut wrenched as he slept, because I knew for a fact that the evidence was in his wallet. I had never looked in his wallet before, and I had always respected his privacy, but I knew that I could no longer trust him. While he slept, I opened his wallet and there was the evidence, a love letter; though brief, it was detailed enough that I no longer questioned my intuition. I couldn't believe that while I lay in the hospital, our "friend" Shirley, who was sending me letters and gifts, was also supporting my husband in ways that were a little too friendly. Clutching the letter I woke Jerry up holding it within inches of his face. I felt betrayed and devastated. Jerry only made one last visit with me to Chuck's office and announced early in the session that the relationship was over.

When we returned home, I asked him for one final attempt at saving our marriage. Maybe if we could get away from everything and talk, the marriage could be saved, so we took a weekend trip to Las Vegas the week before Christmas. He almost backed out at the airport in Reno, but he changed his mind and got on the plane. The trip was awful; Jerry wouldn't go out of the room. He just lay on the bed and wouldn't communicate. All he wanted to do was go home and pack his things. All the while he was smoking cigars and drinking. I spent the entire weekend crying, except when I went to a female impersonator show at one of the hotels. From the Las Vegas airport I called my father, sobbing, telling him that Jerry was leaving me. My dad wanted to talk to him, but I knew that Jerry wouldn't talk to him or to anyone. We flew back to Reno on December 21st. Jerry drove straight home from the airport without saying a word, and as soon as we got home, he packed his bags and left.

This chaos was too much to handle alone. I called my mother and made arrangements to fly home for Christmas. By January 1, 1994, I knew that there would be no reconciliation. As a matter of fact, I decided that I didn't want a reconciliation and that I would be heading back home to Texas. I returned to Reno and informed both Sherrie and Chuck that I would be leaving. My departure date was set for March 1, 1994. I had a lot of work to do before I could leave. I called Jerry and told him my decision. I was surprised that he was shocked and hurt, because he had been refusing to talk to or see me since he moved out.

I called Dr. Forsythe and asked him to order all testing, from blood to bone scans, before March 1st. Next, I asked Jerry if he would meet with me a couple of times to go over a few legal matters that were important. I needed health insurance, so I asked him if he would continue to carry me on his insurance until I could obtain coverage through a job in Texas. Upon his consent, I filed a legal separation agreement which stated that he would maintain my health insurance. This would satisfy the insurance requirements because we were still married.

Next was the matter of the house. My grandparents had loaned me the money to buy the house, and I wanted to make sure that the loan was paid back. I told Jerry that I could care less about any money from the house and would give up my share, but the house would have to be put on the market so my grandparents could be paid. He agreed to these terms, which I also entered into the separation agreement. After I found a job and qualified for insurance, he would file for divorce. This chapter in my life felt like it was now closing.

Chapter 34

Moving Through the Storms

Rejoice in being yourself, a beautiful work of nature, and help
yourself to further growth, that's the best thing.
—Moses Auerbach

As March 1st was getting closer, I was confident that all
the loose ends between Jerry and me had been cleared up.
Now that I had finally recovered from the shock of our
separation, I jumped into taking care of myself. I planned a
slumber party with some of my girlfriends the week before
I left, which was not only great fun but offered a bond of
support in my new adventure. Each day I had lunch or dinner
with a friend, so I could say good-bye. I gave away my
youngest cat, Baby Girl, to a friend who had always wanted
her. I knew that my friend would take good care of Baby
Girl, and I just couldn't take her to Texas because there
wasn't enough room in my car. My sister-in-law had offered
to fly up to Reno and help me drive back if we could swing
by her parents' house on the way back down, and I agreed. I
thought I had everything done. I double-checked my list and
said a prayer.

By now God and I were on good terms, and I was
talking to Him every day. I couldn't help but think back to
that day on the beach when I had found the living, breathing
sand dollar and Jerry had thrown it back into the ocean.
Somehow that event symbolized my life and my freedom,
and I felt Jerry, too, recognized that symbolism on a deeper

level. As he threw the sand dollar back, Jerry released me. Now I could move forward into the future, but if I had been encumbered, I would dry up and be eaten as I remained in the sand. In retrospect, I was able to see the bigger picture. I loaded up my car with my dog, my cat, and my sister-in-law, along with a couple of changes of clothes, and pointed my Toyota southeast towards Texas.

I had shipped the majority of my belongings to my friend's house in Port Aransas, a beach resort town on the Gulf of Mexico in south Texas. Tanya and I hadn't seen each other in many years. She had just bought a three-bedroom house on the beach, and she invited me to move there and live with her. I accepted her offer thinking it would be a nice change.

After a few weeks, even though I liked the beach, I realized that Port Aransas was not the place for me. I asked my brother, Glen, who lived in San Antonio and his wife, Julie, if I could move in with them until I could find a job and a place to live. They graciously said yes, so Glen drove down to Port Aransas, and we loaded my belongings into his four-horse trailer and headed to San Antonio. I had driven up the week before and rented a storage-unit, but when we returned to San Antonio the storage-unit complex had just closed for the evening. Glen suggested that we drive the trailer out to Retama stables where they kept their horses and leave it there until morning. I was nervous about leaving the trailer with all my life's possessions in an unsecured environment, but there weren't too many options that time of night.

When we arrived at the barns, someone had already parked a trailer in Glen's parking place. Glen said, "Not to worry," as he pulled the trailer around and parked it on the dirt access road that ran alongside the first and second barns. Glen jumped out of the truck and said, "I'm going to feed the horses, and I'll be right back." As I watched him enter the pasture where he kept his horses, I began to say a prayer. "God, all my belongings are in this trailer. Would you please take care of them?" And with that I called in the angels as I walked around the trailer, giving thanks and knowing that all would be well. On the way back to the house, Glen and I listened to the weather on the radio. The night was to be a clear night. It had been a long day, so after a late dinner that night, I retired immediately.

I awoke in the night to the most horrific storm. I could hear tornadoes in the storm as the rain and hail came down. I got up and began crying because everything I owned was in the horse trailer. A voice said, "Everything's all right; go back to bed." This voice didn't calm me much. The storm had awakened Julie, also. She came out and tried to console me in her own way. In a Jewish New Jersey accent she said, "Well, there's nothing that you can do, so just go to bed." So, I went back to bed, but I remained awake for the next two hours, listening to the storm. Sunrise came within a few short hours, and I got up to head out to the barns. Julie told me that Glen had already left for the barns and had asked us to wait because he wanted to inspect the damage first. Julie and I waited for almost two hours before he returned.

Glen walked in the door and he didn't say a word. He just stood there shaking his head. I would refer to my brother's beliefs as being similar to those of an atheist's. The first words out of his mouth were, "Beth, someone is looking out for you." He went on to explain that a tornado had hit the barns, had literally ripped the roofs off two of the barns, had partially ripped the roofs off other barns; most of the property was a disaster. The trailer that was parked in his parking place had been completely destroyed, but Glen's trailer didn't have even a scratch on it. He continued, "It was just like a circle had been drawn around my trailer." Some of the metal from the barns had formed a circle three to four feet out from his trailer. Shortly after that, I went out to inspect the damage; it was just as he had said. A few of my things were wet, and I think I lost two pairs of shoes, but that was the extent of my damage. And, of course, his trailer was fine. We worked that day trying to clean up around the barn. For the entire day, Glen walked around shaking his head, all the while repeating that I had very good connections!

Chapter 35

Original Destination

Do not look back in anger, or forward in fear,
but around in awareness.
—James Thurber

Avenues for employment in San Antonio had not manifested after thirty days, so I drove seventy-five miles to Austin and spent the day applying at four different temporary agencies, while also dropping resumes off at different law firms. Within a few hours, one of temporary agencies had work for me in a downtown law firm. I had always wanted to live in Austin, and I had actually planned many years earlier to move there. It looked like now was the time, because the doors of employment were opening for me. The first month, I commuted from San Antonio to Austin because it took a while to find housing that would allow my dog. The commuting made for long days, and I would spend Saturday recovering from fifteen-hour days during the week.

I felt excited and anxious about beginning a new life in a new city. I had been in Austin for a couple of months, and I saw an ad in the Austin Chronicle, an alternative weekly, that promised a fun and relaxed atmosphere to meet new people. A hotel conference room had been rented in Embassy Suites. The program was a question-and-answer game where participants move from group to group. The idea was that the people who had common interests with you would surface in a few of the groups. Toward the conclusion of the evening, the emcee had everyone stop and turn to the closet person, then we were to ask an off-the-cuff question. A woman turned to me and asked, "If you only had one week to live, what would you do?" I smiled and said, "I'd find a cure!" She definitely was not expecting this answer because she looked confused, but I knew what my answer truly meant to me. She had no idea who I was or what I had experienced. I knew when I said these words that it was truth; I'd found a cure through the process of becoming whole and well.

Chapter 36

Collecting the Pieces

*Life is a succession of lessons which
must be lived to be understood.*
–Helen Keller

Now, I know that you think the story ends here, but it doesn't. Even for me, the story has had a surprise ending. As I write this, it has been more than four years since I moved to Austin. I'm in a new relationship and living with a man named Tim, whom I truly love and admire. For the past two summers, we've taken two weeks to travel to different parts of the United States exploring. This last summer, in 1998, Tim and I decided to fly out west to visit friends and relatives that we hadn't seen in many years in California and Nevada. Shortly after he and I met, I learned that he was born at Stanford University Hospital, the same hospital where I had had my bone-marrow transplant. So I told him that I wanted to make time on our trip to go to the hospital, and walk through the CHU floor at Stanford.

Four days after our vacation began, we left San Francisco, heading south towards Palo Alto, California. Upon entering the city, I started to feel anxious, and even before I entered the hospital I could feel my body getting warm. Walking through the hospital doors, my blood pressure shot up and my heart began to beat faster. Tim commented on my face being beet red as we entered the CHU area. I hadn't forgotten where the bone-marrow unit was or CHU, Compromised Host Unit. As I walked around the unit, staff members asked if I needed help. I thanked them and explained that I had been a patient here, five and half years earlier. The staff would smile and let me walk. There was a silent understanding between the CHU staff and patients. I pointed out my room to Tim and explained the different rooms and areas. I asked if Angela, the head nurse, was still there. "No," they said, she had moved on to help open another CHU in another city, along with Dr. Long. I had wanted to say hi to Susie, the nurse who had given me the green knit cap, because I never had a chance to say good-bye, but she worked the night shift and would not be in until after Tim and I had left the hospital. I asked the nurse to leave her a message of "Hi!"

Dr. Blume still ran the Bone-Marrow Program at the hospital, and after asking for directions, I headed towards his office. He wasn't in because he was making rounds. His assistant told me that I could wait for him. I tried to wait, but I walked out of the office explaining that I'd be right back. I ran down the hall crying with Tim beside me asking what was wrong. After I stopped at a stairwell, he just held me while I cried.

I had left a piece of my soul in the hospital. Realizing this, I knew why I had to make this trip back. *To reclaim it!* A prayer of thanks and gratitude came forth. I could feel that portion of my soul return as I began to calm down. I looked up at Tim and said, "Let's go see Dr. Blume."

Dr. Blume was thrilled that I had come by to say hi and took a moment to refresh his memory by looking me up in his files, since he sees hundreds of patients. We sat and talked for a while about what I was doing, and, of course, about how I was feeling. He wanted to know if I was going to be in town during the summer picnic; I wasn't because I would be leaving within a few hours. Dr. Blume called

Trilla, the social worker, into his office. She remembered me and volunteered to take me down to greet some nurses who had been working during my hospitalization. I said good-bye to Dr. Blume as we gave each other another big hug before I followed Trilla. I smiled as I walked out the door, realizing that I forgot he wore bow ties.

Life is about the journey. I have learned that lesson and I continue to encourage myself to follow my heart. I encourage each of you to follow your heart and to do as Jelaluddin Rumi[oo] suggests, *Let the beauty we love be what we do."*

AFTER THOUGHTS

It is my prayer and my greatest wish that all people, young or old, to learn to understand and recognize the inherent wisdom that rests in each individual. Don't wait until a life-threatening illness makes you a statistic before you decide to make changes. Learn to read and trust the markers along the path, so you, too, can make better decisions and live a healthier and happier life. Don't ignore the wisdom that you acquire. To gain health only to disregard it is like putting your head in a hangman's noose and then pulling the lever on the trap door.

Yes, I have my health, and it is still important for me to follow healthy eating habits, as well as being attentive to the road signs along my journey in life. Today I do it not because of fear for my survival, but because I want to live the best way possible. How do you do this? By remembering to listen to your inner voice which is your intuition. Learning to listen takes time to cultivate, so be patient with yourself. The messages are usually subtle, but most people seem to be standing around waiting for the big sign from God, like a building falling on them, before they will wake up. Maybe that's what happened to me. Intuitive messages can come from many sources such as from your dreams, angels, and spirit guides. The messages can also come from unexpected sources such as through the radio, or from a new friend, or eaves-dropping on a conversation, or simply from quieting your mind for a moment. But what is guaranteed is that you will have an opportunity to look at the many aspects of relationships, and most importantly the relationship to yourself.

SUMMARY OUTLINE

This chapter is to assist anyone who is interested in what I did at a quick glance. In some areas this outline includes more specific information on steps or processes which I mentioned in the book. The following list delineates how I used both alternative and traditional methods to create a new complementary approach to healing, which has become a part of my life. If you need further information, you are welcome to call or write me at Violet Crown Publishing, P. O. Box 3107, Austin, Texas 78764, (512) 707-9886, fax: (512) 441-2233, and e-mail: shaktiB@aol.com.

I wish to make it clear that I do not recommend total rejection of orthodox methods of treating illness, or of a doctor's advice. If you are ill, see your doctor. I am not a physician or a psychologist and do not purport to be one. None of the following information is for the purpose of diagnosing, treating, alleviating, mitigating, curing, preventing, or caring for "disease" in any way or manner whatsoever. All teachings and methods are for the sole purpose of assisting people to learn how to build their own health.

Also please know that many of the methods listed, although they may focus mainly on one part of the body, mind, or spirit trinity, they actually work on all three. For instance, if you are working on improving your physical health, you end up also healing your mind and spirit. Why? Because life is about working together, and this cooperation, both among the parts of ourselves and with other people opens us to healing on all levels.

BODY

Dr. Reams' Program: Vitamin/Mineral and Dietary program. Saliva and urine was tested weekly to monitor my vitamin intake. The diet consisted of a combination of vegetarianism and macrobiotics. Parasite cleanses and herbs were also used, such as blood purifying teas, i.e., Jason Winter's Tea, Essiac Tea.

Colonics: A high enema. Check your local phone book for listings for colonic irrigation therapists. You can also write to Eldon Lowder, Western Health Research, 7835 D, 1300 E., Sandy, Utah 84092, for a colonic board that you can use at home. The Jason Winters Story claims this board is "easy to use, good for the whole family, and sells for around $200, so it pays for itself in just a couple of weeks."

Lemon Water and Distilled Water: Part of Dr. Reams' program. The recipe is as follows: begin the day with one quart of lemon water and one quart of distilled water. To make the lemon water, use the juice of three lemons and fill the quart container with water. You may add maple syrup if you desire. First thing in the morning drink 4 oz of lemon water, and then thirty minutes later, drink 4 oz of distilled or purified water. Continue throughout the day every thirty minutes alternating the lemon water and plain water. This creates a slow continual flush of toxins from the body and liver.

Castor Oil Packs: Edgar Cayce recommended Castor oil packs to facilitate healing; refer to his books or to Chapter 6 in this book for more information.

Chiropractic: Keeping the spine and skeletal structure

aligned produces an increase in the circulation of bodily fluids, and improves the function of the nervous system. The improvement of the skeletal and nervous systems aides in the detoxification of the body, and, therefore, more rapid healing. I also had cranial adjustments during the time of laetrile injections. The cranial adjustments facilitated proper drainage of the sinus cavities and lymphatic system. Check your local phone book for chiropractors.

Liver/Gallbladder Flush: I do a good liver and gallbladder flush once a year. The flush needs to be done under supervision of a health care professional. If you would like a copy of my recipe for the liver and gallbladder flush, please send $5.00 to Violet Crown Publishing, P. O. Box 3107, Austin, Texas 78764. Please allow for two weeks for delivery.

Fasting: Abstaining from food has been used for years in religious observances but is also used to allow the digestive tract a chance to rest and to promote accelerated cleansing of toxins within the system. There are many types of fasts. I have used three-day water, watermelon or fruit, and vegetable juice fasts. The fruit or vegetable juice fasts are easier both physically and mentally and will provide easily digested nutrients for the body, as well as keeping energy levels higher.

Raw Juices: Just as raw juices are beneficial in supplying nutrients to the body during fasting, they are great for you on a daily basis. It is best to drink the juice fresh (by fresh I mean within fifteen to thirty minutes of juicing). There are many fruits and vegetables to choose from in juicing. Some of my favorites are: orange/apple, orange/pineapple, carrot, carrot/celery, and carrot/beet/spinach.

Barley Green, Spirulina, Wheat Grass: These substances supply the body with needed nutrients, such as minerals, enzymes, and chlorophyll. You can find several different kinds at your local health food store. Now I mostly use Spirulina instead of Barley Green. You can also drink the raw juice of wheat grass. To obtain information on wheat grass, read Ann Wigmore's books or contact the Optimum Health Institute in San Diego, California.

Walking/Exercise: Walking a mile or more a day increases oxygen levels in the blood steam. I used walking and swimming as the main sources of exercise during the ten years. Any kind of daily exercise is good for you. Try walking, swimming, bicycling, rollerblading, jumping on a trampoline, etc.

Hellerwork/Rolfing: Both of these techniques are types of deep massage that break down the rigidity of the Fascial tissue, correcting the muscular structure of the body and releasing emotional traumas that are stored in the tissues. Because the muscular structures holds the skeletal structure in place, it's important for the whole alignment of the body to release the miscellaneous trauma. Look under massage in your local phone book.

Psychic Surgery: I used psychic surgery right before my transplant and right after the transplant. I now have a yearly healing session as maintenance. Psychic surgery is a type of healing that heals on physical, emotional, and spiritual levels.Many people organize trips to the Philippines to see psychic surgeons. Occasionally some Philippine healers travel to the U.S.

Hydrogen Peroxide: In the beginning I used diluted thirty-five percent food-grade hydrogen peroxide to increase the oxygen levels in my body since over the years oxygen levels in the atmosphere have been dropping. Today I use magnesium oxide, which is easier on the body and more beneficial because you can take higher amounts (Dr. Donsbach's magnesium oxide). Unless you have done extensive research and know exactly how to administer the thirty-five percent food-grade hydrogen peroxide, do not use it because it can cause liver damage.

Shark Cartilage: Shark cartilage is being used in the treatment of cancer and arthritis. Some doctors today are even having patients use the cartilage along with chemotherapy. In studies outside the United States, shark cartilage has been shown be to more beneficial than chemotherapy in the elimination of cancerous tumors. The benefits of shark cartilage are not as recognized here in the States, because according to the FDA, only a drug can cure, and shark cartilage is considered a food supplement. Refer to the book reference section for author and title.

Colloidal Silver: A pre-1938 drug that was used as a natural antibiotic and anti-inflammatory. It is known to kill more than 650 viruses, infections and diseases. It can kill a germ within six minutes of contact. Colloidal silver works as a second immune system in the body. It has been used in treatments ranging from AIDS to cancer and many more. It can be obtained through health food stores and multi-level distributing companies.

Asparagus and Vitamin C: This recipe came to me through a couple of sources and seems to regenerates healthy cells faster than the diseased cells. I take two bundles of fresh asparagus and lightly steam it; after steaming I puree it and store it in glass in the refrigerator. Every day for two weeks I eat three tablespoons of the puree three times a day. About every three days you will need to make more asparagus puree. During the two-week period of ingesting asparagus, I also increase my buffered, powdered vitamin C intake to 10,000 mg a day divided into four dosages of 2,500 mg each.

Parsley Tea: Parsley has been used as a tumor-growth inhibitor and as an aphrodisiac. Take a cup of parsley and put it in a pint of boiling water. Turn off and steep for two hours for the tumor-growth inhibitor; and steep for forty-five minutes for the aphrodisiac. The tea tastes best warm.

Laetrile/Vitamin Injections: I had daily IV drips of laetrile and vitamins for a period of two months and then bi-weekly for a period of 3 months. There are laetrile clinics and vitamin injection clinics around the country.

Herbs: I use herbs and herbal teas when needed. You will need to research which herbs would be appropriate for you. Refer to the book reference section or your local bookstore for titles of herbal books.

Massage/Bodywork: Massage helps to relax the body and mind and to energize and oxygenate the body. Check locally for massage therapists and bodyworkers. There are many different types of massage and Bodywork, such as Swedish, Deep Tissue, Shiatsu, Reflexology, and Accupressure. It is important to do some research and find out which kind you are drawn to.

Breath work: Both exercise and breath work increase the oxygen in the body. There are many different types of breath work. One that I like to use daily is alternate breathing. To do alternate breathing, close the right nostril with the right thumb and inhale through the left nostril. Then close the left nostril with the index or middle finger of the right hand, remove the thumb and exhale through the right nostril. Then inhale through the right nostril, and close it with the thumb, and exhale through the left nostril. In the beginning do this six times, increasing until you are able to do it twelve times twice a day. Best to do in the shower.

Reiki: Reiki is an energy healing which balances the energy in the physical and ethereal bodies. It is a hands-on healing technique and can be very powerful in healing the body, mind, and spirit. You can refer to Chapter 7 for more information. Check your local phone book for Reiki practitioners.

Color Therapy: Color-and-light therapy has been used for centuries. Projection of colored light on the body is used for healing, or you can charge water with the colors and take it internally. You can also eat foods of a certain color, thereby ingesting the energy of that color or use the colors in clothing and imagery. You can take this still further with the use of gems, crystals, and stones of various colors to clear and heal both the physical and energy field. The exploration of color and its many uses is fascinating and is essential. In the color section you will find further information about the different colors.

Chemotherapy: A treatment of disease with chemicals which have a specific toxic effect on both the disease-producing micro-organism and the healthy cells. I underwent chemotherapy treatments for approximately four years. Your oncologist will have information on chemotherapy and its side effects. Be sure to also ask your pharmacist and check in your local bookstore for further information.

Radiation: The emission and spreading of radioactive particles or waves to specific areas of the body for killing cancerous cells. The only time I agreed to radiation therapy was during my bone marrow transplant. Be sure to ask your physician and check in your local bookstore for further information.

Bone-Marrow Transplant: A bone-marrow transplant is a very aggressive form of traditional therapy. Depending on the type of transplant, either your own marrow will be used or you will need a bone-marrow donor. The procedure includes the use of chemotherapy and radiation in very high dosages to completely kill off both healthy and diseased cells, so that the good, healthy, sterilized cells, the bone marrow that was harvested earlier, can be injected into your system for a fresh start or new beginning. Be sure to ask your physician and check in your local bookstore for further information.

MIND

Reading: Books on self-improvement, encouragement, inspiration, health, healing, and angels are all beneficial in keeping you knowledgeable and uplifted. Refer to the reading reference section of this book for titles.

Visualization: In using visualization in conjunction with treating disease, you can create imagery that will break down and dissolve the illness, removing illness and tumors from the body. Visualization is great to use even when your healthy because it can strengthen the body. Mediation tapes can be found at your local bookstores, and there are many tapes to choose from, or you can make up your own. You may want to write down a specific visualization that you would like to use, and then tape record it, so you can relax and listen to it later. During the visualizations you will find yourself able to more easily meet spiritual teachers or healers who can help you with messages and information.

Support Groups: One of the support groups I attended was Beyond Illness a cancer group based on Bernie Siegel's program. Check with your doctor, local hospital, or other organizations for support groups in your area.

Self-Improvement Courses or Seminars: Bernie Siegel offers seminars around the country, at both health shows and medical centers. There are many programs or courses that can help, such as A Course In Miracles and Maxine Cardinal's course The Wonderful World of Miracles. Choose programs that teach you how to travel through life with a positive attitude while being an active participate.

Flower Essences: Bach Flowers, Deva Flowers, Perelandra. Flower essences help to balance the emotions so you can deal with the trauma or emotion without stressing. Bach Flowers and Deva Flowers remedies are sold in stores around the nation. Perelandra can be reached by writing to Box 136, Jeffersonton, Virginia 22724.

Professional Counseling: Therapy should be considered when you are dealing with a serious health condition; I used it through many stages of my treatment. The primary time during which I received counseling was while preparing for and while undergoing the bone-marrow transplant. I continued my sessions for a few months after the transplant while I was adjusting to normal. Check with your doctor or phone book for local therapists.

Dreams: I had studied dreams in college, and I have continued to study and work with my dreams since 1983. Dreams offer insight into the condition of your health, messages from your angels, and help with sorting out everyday concerns. Check your local bookstore for dream interpretation books, and check for local dream-interpretation classes. There are many forms of interpretation — you are your best guide. Dreams are your personal connecion to your subconscious.

Toning/ Vocalization: We internalize many things throughout our lives (pain, secrets, joy). Toning involves using a series of sounds that help your mind and body release old, damaging thoughts from childhood and later stages of life while at the same time recharging the body and soul. To completely empty yourself of the past and move into the future you must learn to express your pain and joy with exuberance. Putting sound to emotions stops the process of holding them inside, and the release creates a healthier life.

SPIRIT

Prayer: I have always used prayer. This is a personal decision, but if you've never tried praying, I recommend it. Prayer is the gift of asking God or spirit for what you desire; mediation is the gift of listening to the answers.

Mediation: I have used meditation for more than twenty years. I often listen to mediation tapes as I lie down to sleep. There are hundreds of types of meditation — you will need to do some research to find the right type for yourself. There is probably a meditation group in your area. The purpose of meditation is to quiet the mind and still the spirit, allowing the spirit to be present in the body and opening you to the voice of God.

Reading: Inspirational reading helps the body to continually move forward by nurturing the spirit within.

Toning/Vocalization: (Described further on page 168)

Church: If you can find a church that you resonate with, attending it can be very supportive, both spiritually and socially.

Baptism: It was important for me to be rebaptized right before the bone-marrow transplant. The baptism was a spiritual ceremony to prepare my mind and spirit for the long and hard process I was about to go through. The baptism for me was like having my battery charged.

Psychic Surgery: Heals the body, mind, and spirit.

Visualization: (Described further on page 166)

Remember to look to all areas for support, including friends, support groups, reading, education, volunteer work, prayer lists, etc.

COLORS

Colors have the ability to make us feel happy or sad. I know that my mood determines my choice of clothing when I look into my closet or dresser each day. If I don't feel good, I may grab something drab, but if I feel happy, I want something brighter and cheerier. Well, just as you choose colors for moods, you can choose colors to help assist you in healing.

The following list provides some information on certain colors and their uses:

RED is a warm, stimulating color that has maybe one of the largest lists of uses. It will improve circulation and stimulate the senses and the entire body. I find that it works like a tonic on the body. It is not advised for use if there is already inflammation or fevers. Red foods: beets, tomatoes, radishes, watermelon.

PINK is a mental color and is considered a universal healing color which can raise the vibration of the body, but it is not advised for people who have trouble sleeping or who are highly excitable. Pink foods: pink grapefruit, guava.

ORANGE is a body normalizer and can increase the calcium in your body. It can be used in the treatment of diseases that are due to the depletion of or the misplacement of calcium in the body. Orange brings vitality, energy, and enthusiasm. If you don't like orange, learn to like it or wear it under your clothing in the form of underwear or T-shirts. Orange foods: carrots, sweet potatoes, pumpkin, oranges, tangerines, butternut squash, cantaloupes.

YELLOW helps to relieve constipation, strengthen the nervous system, eliminate parasites, and eliminate mucus from the body. Yellow food: corn, banana, pineapples, lemons, honeydew melons.

GREEN increases vitality and health, nourishes the entire body, stimulates the pituitary, dissolves blood clots, and eliminates toxins from the body. Green deals a lot with balancing the body so it can be used to increase vitality and decrease illness or disease where needed. Green foods: broccoli, green beans, bell pepper, cabbage, kale, spinach, mustard greens, chard. When choosing green food in the grocery store you need to pick the darkest, richest color.

BLUE is a calming and soothing color. It has even been used to calm and quiet violent behavior in criminals. The color blue can be used to reduce fevers, inflammation, and pain. Blue foods: blueberries.

PURPLE and its family of colors help in building the blood and white blood cells, as well as helping with sleeping disorders. Drinking a glass of grape juice before bed will help you to sleep better. Because the violets, purples, and indigos are so good in the treatment of the blood, they are found to be very useful in the treatment of heart ailments.

WHITE and the many shades of white are considered to be of the highest vibration. White is purifying, uplifting, and can help increase the ability to handle high levels of stress as the soul is unfolding within life's challenges."It is considered to vibrate with all colors.

BROWN is symbolic of the earth and represents the growth, effort, and wish to accomplish. You can use brown to get your life more organized. Too much brown in your life can connect into a inner belief that life has to be difficult.

GRAY/BLACK can indicate a heaviness, dullness, or illness. People who wear a lot of gray or black are often loners. It's okay to live life according to your own rules, but it's not healthy to shut others out completely, so be sure to add a little color to your life.

BOOK REFERENCES

CANCER and DISEASE

Diamond, Harvey. You Can Prevent Breast Cancer!
California: ProMotion Publishing, 1995. ••

Diamond, John W., Lee W. Cowden, Burton Goldberg.
Definitive Guide to Cancer: Cancer can be Reversed.
(This Book Tells How, Using Clinically Proven
Complementary and Alternative Therapies.) California:
Future Medicine Publishing, Inc., 1997.

Lane, William I. and Linda Comac. Sharks Don't Get
Cancer: How Shark Cartilage Could Save Your Life. New
York: Avery Publishing Group Inc., 1992.

Sattilaro, Anthony J. and Tom Monte. Recalled By Life.
New York: Avon Books, 1982.

Siegel, Bernie S. Love, Medicine & Miracles: Lessons
Learned About Self-Healing From a Surgeon's Experience
With Exceptional Patients. New York: Harper & Row,
1988.

Willner, Robert E. Deadly Deception: The Proof That Sex
and HIV Absolutely DO NOT CAUSE AIDS. Florida:
Peltec Publishing Co., Inc., 1994.

Winters, Jason. The Four Best Selling Natural Health
Books Now Under One Cover! "Killing Cancer," "In
Search of the Perfect Cleanse," "Breakthrough," "The
Ultimate Combination." Nevada: Vinton Publishing, 1990.

NUTRITIONAL and DIETARY

Airola, Paavo. How to Get Well: Dr. Airola's Handbook of Natural Healing. Oregon: Health Plus, 1993.

Kulvinskas, Viktoras, H. Survival into the 21st Century: Planetary Healers Manual. Connecticut: 21st Century Publications, 1975.

Northrup, Christiane. Women's Bodies, Women's Wisdom: Creating Physical and Emotional Health and Healing. New York: Bantam Books, 1998.

Pitchford, Paul. Healing with Whole Foods: Oriental Traditions and Modern Nutrition. California: North Atlantic Books, 1993.

Rector-Page. Linda, Healthy Healing: An Alternative Healing Reference. California: Spillman Printing, 1989.

Shank, Chik. Alternatives in Healing, Nutrition, Consciousness. Florida: Alternatives, 1978.

JUICES and FASTING

Brandt, Johanna. The Grape Cure. New York: Ehret Literature Publishing Co., Inc.

Walker, N.W. Fresh Vegetable and Fruit Juices: What's Missing in your Body? Arizona: Norwalk Press, 1970.

Shelton, Herbert M. Fasting Can Save Your Life. Florida: American Natural Hygiene Society, Inc., 1993

COOKBOOKS

Kendall, Frances. Sweet Temptations Natural Dessert Book. New York: Avery Publishing Group Inc., 1988

Vegetarian Times. Vegetarian Times Complete Cookbook. New York: MacMillan, 1995

Katzen, Mollie. Vegetable Heaven. New York: Hyperion, 1997.

Pitchford, Paul. Healing with Whole Foods: Oriental Traditions and Modern Nutrition. California: North Atlantic Books, 1993.

HERBS and FOLKLORE

Arvigo, Rosita. My Apprenticeship with a Maya Healer: SATSUN. San Francisco: Harper 1994.

Pat Little Dog. Border Healing Woman. Texas: University of Texas Press, Austin, 1985.

Lust, John. The Herb Book: The Most Complete Catalog of Nature's "Miracle Plants' Ever Published. Toronto: Bantam Books, 1974.

Vogel, A. Swiss Nature doctor: An Encyclopedic Collection of Helpful Hints Gathered From the Swiss Folklore of Natural Healing. Switzerland: A. Vogel, 1980

DREAM BOOKS

Bro, Harmon Hartzell. Edgar Cayce On Dreams. New York: Warner Books, 1968.

Faraday, Ann, Ph.D. The Dream Game. New York: Harper & Row, 1974

Hall, Calvin S. The Meaning of Dreams. New York: McGraw-Hill Book Company, 1966.

Mahoney, Maria F. The Meaning in Dreams and Dreaming. New Jersey: The Citadel Press, 1966.

Quinn, Adrienne. Dreams: Secret Messages From Your Mind. Washington: Dream Research, 1985.

ALTERNATIVE SCIENCES IN HEALING

Quantum Physics

Chopra, Deepak. Ageless Body, Timeless Mind: The Quantum Alternative to Growing Old. New York: Harmony Books, 1993. ••

Color and Energy Therapy

Clark, Linda. The Ancient Art of Color Therapy. New York: Simon & Schuster, 1975.

Bruyere, Rosalyn L. Wheels of Light: Chakras, Auras, and the Healing Energy of the Body. New York: Simon & Schuster, 1994.

Burroughs, Stanley. Healing for the Age of Enlightenment. California: Stanley Burroughs, 1976.

Hay, Louise L. Your Can Heal Your Life. California: Hay House, 1984.

Joy, W. Brugh. Joy's Way: A map for the Transformational Journey; An Introduction to the Potentials for Healing with Body Energies. New York: Jeremy P. Tarcher/Putnam, 1979.

Reflexology

Ingham, Eunice D. Stories the Feet Can Tell Thru Reflexology: Stories the Feet Have Told Thru Reflexology. Florida: Ingham Publishing, Inc., 1984.

Iridology

Jensen, Bernard. The Science and Practice of Iridology. California: Bernard Jensen enterprises, 1989.

Toning and Music

Keyes, Laurel Elizabeth. Toning: The Creative Power of the Voice. California: DeVorss & Co., 1990.

McClellan, Randall. The Healing Forces of Music, History, Theory & Practice. Massachusetts: Element, Inc., 1991.

Crystals and Healing

Mella, Dorothee L. Stone Power: Now you can make the Hidden Energies in Gems and Crystals Work for You! New York: Warner Books, 1986.

The Mind and Healing

Myss, Caroline. Why People Don't Heal and How They Can. New York: Harmony Books, 1997.

Silva, Jose and Robert B. Stone. You The Healer: The World-Famous Silva Method on How To Heal Yourself and Others. New York: Instant Improvement, Inc., 1989.

Exercise

Truman, Karol Kuhn and Alan Parkinson. Looking Good Feeling Great: Fifteen Minutes a Day to a New You! An easy, fun way to tone your figure, improve health, develop total fitness! Utah: Olympus Distributing, 1984.

INSPIRATIONAL

Bach, Richard. Illusions: the Adventures of a Reluctant Messiah . New York: Dell 1977. **

Burnham, Sophy. A Book of Angels. New York: Ballantine Books, 1990.

Canfield, Jack and Mark Victor Hansen. Chicken Soup for the Soul: 101 Stories to Open the Heart and Rekindle the Spirit. Florida: Health Communications, Inc. 1993. **

Daniel, Alma, Timothy Wyllie, and Andrew Ramer. Ask Your Angels: A Practical Guide to Working with the Messengers of Heaven to Empower and Enrich Your Life. New York: Ballantine Books, 1992.

Frankel, Lois. Kindling THE SPIRIT: Acts of Kindness and Words of Courage for Women. Florida: Health Communications, Inc., 1994.

Fox, Emmet. Find and Use Your Inner Power or "Sparks of Truth." San Francisco: Harper & Row, 1979. ••

Millman, Dan. Way of The Peaceful Warrior: A book That Changes Lives. California: H.J. Kramer, Inc., 1984. ••

———The Warrior Athlete: Body, Mind & Spirit. New Hampshire: Stillpoint Publishing, 1979. ••

Spalding, Baird T. Life and Teaching of the Masters of the Far East: Volumes 1 - 5. California: DeVorss & Co., 1964.

Sugrue, Thomas. The Story Of Edgar Cayce: There is a River. Virginia: A.R.E. Press, 1973. ••

•• *Any books by this author are suggested as good reading.*

How to Reach the Author

Beth Carpenter gives lectures and workshops internationally. If you wish to contact her for information on her lectures, workshops, or private counseling sessions; and scheduling for radio or television shows, please contact Violet Crown Publishing at (512) 707-9886, by fax at (512) 441-2233, by e-mail: shaktiB@aol.com or you can write to her at Violet Crown Publishing, Attn. Beth Carpenter, P.O. Box 3107, Austin, Texas, 78764.